DR. EUGENE UNDERWOOD

Building A Firm Foundation

Contents

Dedication

I dedicate this book to a wonderful young lady who is now in heaven, my daughter. As I watched her suffer the last days of her life as she let cancer rip through her body, I learned a lot about her and her king. It was this mystery of suffering I saw the father employ during sickness and disease that he allows for a much higher purpose. It appears at the on-set that the one who is dying is losing, but at closer examination nothing can be farther from the truth. When the father told me concerning my daughter that "for this cause she came into the world to become seed for my last day's army", I was not ready to hear that about my only daughter. She had only been married then for a few years and had no children, but died at the age of 33. He called her a martyr because she allowed her life to be taken at his will not hers that she surrendered too. As she lay dying she rose up in the bed and forcefully took my hands off her body and told me to quit praying. I told her no and waited until she fell asleep to resume praying. She did it several times during the night, then the Lord spoke to me and said "Let her go". I told him no, this is my only daughter and I can't do that because it would hurt too much. He said to me, "I have convinced her to come home", and he could not take her at her faith level now. I must let go. But I refused and for several days they both wore me down demanding I let go. After I cried to the Lord that he really needed to help me , I relented and let her go. She died the next day. As she took her last breath the spirit of prophecy fell upon me as her mother, husband, and five brothers stood there and cried until we could cry no more. I began to speak "She has qualified to join the Joel 2 army". I did not know what that fully meant, so I returned home that night in prayer crying to the Lord about what just happened. He said, "Because she went early the way she did the suffering qualified her to step into glory at a greater level and degree of glory which perfected the greater love in her. Because of this she will be returning to the earth in the last days with a whole army of youth from heaven that will join the army of youth on the earth to finish the last day's battle." This same suffering is supposed to happen to the average Christian as they overcome the flesh and nail it to the cross, which produces a great level of internal suffering when we focus on the unseen and not the seen. I know what I am saying will be hard for many to understand because this mystery has not been taught in the church as it was during the early church. In Hebrews it says many of the saints refuse to escape from death so that they might have a better resurrection. What can be better than just simply dying in the faith or at a ripe old age, martyrdom.

I watched this same thing happen to my mother but under different circumstances. My mother got very sick and kept it from her children and would not go to the hospital so some of my sisters did not take her. I told my younger sister you'd better take my mom to the doctor or I'm coming down there and hurt all of you. My younger sister took her and she was operated on but what they took eventually came back just like my daughter. When I found out I called my mother and talked to her about her salvation and readiness to leave but I also preached to her the word of faith. After completing the message I gave her, she said to me, "Yea, yea, I know what you're saying but this was put on me." I repeated to her several times what I was saying to assure her that God doesn't put sickness on people after which she repeated,"Yea, yea, but it was put on me." After several tries and frustration I gave up and hung up. Of course checking up on her over a several month period until I got that dreadful call that mom was dying. She had gone from about 135 pounds to 80 pounds when I saw her again. I flew from Alaska to Memphis and laid upon her bedroom floor for three days crying out to the Lord to heal my mom and why he should. I stated forth my cause and later he spoke and stated his.

Isaiah 43:25-26

25 I, even I, am he that blotteth out thy transgressions for mine own sake, and will not remember thy sins.

26 Put me in remembrance: let us plead together: declare thou, that thou mayest be justified.

The Lord began to speak, "I'm trying to do what you asked me". I said, "Lord what do you mean she is dying and you're not healing her". Then he reminded me by the spirit of several conversations I had with my mom and with him about my mom. I had said to him over the years Lord I want my mom to grow spiritually but I know she is not going to come out of that dead church her husband had started many years before, who is now dead. I said what you mean, he said this is not just about death it is about how you die, are you ready to die. Then he reminded me of the conversation I had with her about healing and she kept on saying it was put on me. The Lord then said to me she didn't know your lingo, she didn't know to say it was permitted on me the same way it was with Job. As with Job he was brought into a higher place through promotion, as the case with mom it was a promotion into glory. So he said to me when she died she would die at a greater degree and level of glory had I not allowed this. I wept and wept not because of my loss but my mom's gain. So my mom and my daughter, different circumstances but the same method to accomplish our fathers purpose. However I know most in the body will not go that route, the normal route is to overcome sin in the flesh by dying to self while being broken, hence internal suffering. Which builds the character of Christ within our eternal souls.

Foreward

I am much delighted that our dear brother, Dr. Eugene Underwood, has written this wonderful book. I have known our dear brother since 2001. He has been a faithful, truthful, and dedicated servant of God. He has strived to live righteously and holy before our Lord God. He has also maintained a cordial and approachable relationship with his fellow ministers of God.

In this book, our dear brother has attempted to write on a subject that is basic to the Christian faith, yet it needs retelling. Most Christians keep falling and fumbling over with the basics time after time. So, this book is a timely reminder to get back to the basics and most vital truths to Christianity.

The author has articulated his thoughts and penned them in a simple and concise manner for all-new as well as older Christians to understand and grasp the truths and apply them in their lives. The author has written beautifully on the Sermon on the Mount, making it readable, understandable, and applicable in our lives.

I pray this book will be a great blessing to the body of Christ.

Sadhu Sundar Selvaraj

Jesus Ministries

Introduction

Having a Good Foundation

In Hebrews, Paul wrote about not wasting time rebuilding a foundation that should have already been laid in your life.

> ### Hebrews 6:1-2
> Therefore leaving the principles of the doctrine of Christ, let us go on unto perfection; not laying again the foundation of repentance from dead works, and of faith toward God,2 Of the doctrine of baptisms, and of laying on of hands, and of resurrection of the dead, and of eternal judgment.

He then admonishes them to go on unto perfection. You cannot keep doing the same thing over and over and over again. That means before you build you have to make sure you have a good foundation.

One of the problems with living in third world nations is with their building structures. Because of the mixture or low quality of cement that is in so many of their structures, when an earthquake takes place their buildings fall so easily. I thank God for what we have in America called building codes.

We have building codes today because they have learned in the past that if you do not build a certain way, it will cause structures to collapse.Consequently, because of this quality control inspectors look for inferior materials. They look for material that is not up to par whether it be wood, lumber or cement. So, whatever the case may be when they find materials that do not have the quality that is needed, it is subject to erosion. In the case of wood, they have a fire-retardant spray that they spray on the wood to lengthen the life of the wood. And in the same way with cement, they have elements that are added to strengthen the solidity of the cement to ensure the life of the building.

In the natural, we take many steps to ensure that the quality of our natural possessions will have a long life, but when it comes to our spiritual life, we do very little to make sure that what we are doing will bring forth lasting, abundant good fruit and that our efforts are not for nothing.

If we are thinking from a building perspective, when it comes to spiritual things everything that we build with, which is the Word of God, is in the foundation itself, with Christ our Lord being the Chief Cornerstone. Keep in mind the importance of the Life of Christ in every stone that is being laid within you. Christ our Lord is the chief corner stone that plums the line in both directions of your life, he is not the entire foundation in the beginning. Just as the seed must burst forth from its shell which represents your flesh and come forth from the dirt which is your soul. And by its fruit fill your garden which ye are, likewise each stone laid by you must be filled with his life. He only builds with Zoe life so each preceding one must be like unto the first one.

Therefore, some of you that read this book will find out that all that has been built upon must be torn down. You have others whose foundation has not been properly laid and everything you have built must be torn down alone with the foundation being ripped up and relayed. Then there are others who must do all they can to maintain their foundation so that it does not erode, just like a natural foundation would and make sure the substance from which you are building are of the same life as his. Building with the proper substance upon the proper foundation will ensure the strengthening of your foundation that is laid. Our Lord in the sermon on the mount teaches of the substance of his character that must be in the builder or sower and the ways it is accomplished.

So, if we know anything about laying a foundation, whether it be with cement blocks or poured cement, the person laying the blocks will drop a plumb line to make sure the foundation that is about to be laid is straight or square. Because if you are off even by an 1/8 of an inch, it will cause the foundation to be out of alignment. The higher you build, the more It will be off. It is the same way with the Lord. If you start building a foundation that is not secure, that has mixture, that is not like the first stone you laid, which is the Lord, the longer you are in the Kingdom the farther you will get off. In retrospect to enduring or lasting as a believer in this world the bible speaks about two main principles. The parable of the sower or the man that built his house, each speaks to the overcomer's life and you growing up in the kingdom of God. However, in this book we will approach it more from the basics of the hindrances you will encounter from your sowing or building or rather how God has chosen to develop you. The end results being a firm foundation and the character of our King.

Godly Character

When we talk about Godly character as a Christian, those things must be a part of our foundation. As a newborn in Christ, those things tend to elude us because we do not make the main thing the main thing, which is God's character. Christ Our Lord had 30 years of filling His character with the fruit of the spirit just to do three and a half years of ministry. The love that we walk in as a newborn believer is very weak, we are still living a selfish and self-centered life, where we only think of ourselves. The joy that we have is not the joy of the Lord. Our lives consist in the abundance of things we possess. We find happiness in what we own and what we have as a Christian, and not by having Christ on the inside of us. There is very little Godly character that is oozing from us as a Christian.

But grace plays a big part of dealing with the mixture that is in our lives. For God looks at the slack and lack according to our spiritual age and He grades us accordingly. Just like we do with children. When we raise our children, we expect more out of a 13-year-old than we do from a three-year-old. We give the three-year-old more slack. When a three-year-old comes and takes our prized possession off the shelf we do not slap the three-year old on the bottom and say NO! We take that moment as a teaching lesson and put it out of their reach, because we know they are not going to listen at that age. But if our 13-year-old does the same thing, they might get a slap because we expect more from them.

To Whom Much is Given, Much is Required

God is no different. He says in His word that to whom much is given, much is required. So, we have to understand this spiritual wisdom and principle. That we cannot gage one another, or grade one another so to speak, because God has the scorecard and we cannot judge where someone stands with Him. Have you ever noticed someone who's walking with the Lord and how they get away with stuff that we may not? The Lord may jump on our case because to whom much is given, much is required. The scripture says that when we come into the Light, when we see truth that we are to walk therein. It says nothing about if we feel like it, or if we are up to it, but to walk therein. It is a commandment to walk therein.

Because of our spiritual age we may not be capable, but within our foundation – within the mixture – the mortar, whatever we want to call it, we have been given the grace that we need to do so! So, grace is flowing within us and it enables us to stand. At the same time, God looks individually according to our spiritual age and He expects more from us when we know better. As Christians, we are supposed to be growing, but sadly many are not, especially when they hear truth. Instead, many choose to not walk in the Light of that truth. When that happens, we need to understand that God will still be measuring our spiritual age according to what it should be. Meaning, we will start finding very little grace mixed within the compounds of our lives.

We will find that our Father will employ tests and trials to encourage us to change the course of direction in our lives, wanting them to come back into alignment with His perfect ways. If we do not change our ways, He will stop protecting us from some of the messes still in our lives, and we will be drawn away in our own lust without grace to drive us to our knees to point out that we can do nothing without Him.

It is like once our child starts to walk and we see that they are getting battered and bruised, because they are hitting the wall all the time. So, we run to the store and buy knee pads, helmets, and everything else to stop them from getting hurt. But when we see that is not working, we pick them up and say, "I will never put you down and let you try to walk again." We are not that stupid as a parent, right? No, we are not, instead, we just make sure we stay a little bit closer to them while they learn to walk. And because we are a little bit closer, they have fewer bruises when they fall down. But as parents we know that they have to learn to walk and that bruises are a part of life. However, in the house of God there are many who are still holding very big bottles and have not learned to walk yet.

Learn to Rely on His Abilities

We tend to think God is like humans, but when God lets us fall on our blessed assurance and feel the pain of our stupidity, of our lethargy and of our laziness, we do not realize often that is what He is doing. That is exactly what He is wanting us to feel! Not because He wants to shame us, but because He wants us to learn humility and to rely on His abilities, and not our own. Instead, though, we try to force God's hands with statements like, "He knows what I need" as if He can take the initiative without us. But He cannot and He will not!

That is why the Bible says in the world we will have tribulation. We are going to have troubles. We are going to have pain and go through hard times. Christ our Lord went on to say, *"Be of good cheer,"* because He is the blueprint and has given us the road map on how to walk in this world that is full of tribulation, so that we will come out the other side successful.

Christ our Lord is telling us in this Christian walk, while we are building our foundation, that we are going to miss it. We are going to mess up and we are going to fall on our face. We are going to even feel like quitting at times. But Christ our Lord is there as a loving heavenly Father to lift us up, if we want to be picked up. He is there to help us to move forward, if we want His help to move forward.

Heaven supplies everything that we need to be successful. The problem with Christians today is either they are not following the blueprint or they are veering off the path that God placed them on trying to do their own thing. We have to look at this from two perspectives. There is the truth that is written in God's Word, within the foundation, that will make us what we are. At the same time, there is also within the foundation the purpose for which we are here, and the purpose for which He created us. And the more we mature in truth, the clearer it will become why we are here.

Disciplining Our Flesh

Our purpose and destiny become clearer because they are intertwined. This is why the Bible calls us Christians first at Antioch (Acts 11:26). They were the ones who exercised discipline to live a righteous life. If someone who calls themselves a Christian is not disciplining their flesh or not putting pressure on their flesh, the enemy will. The enemy wants to put pressure on us through our flesh, but we need to learn to put pressure on our flesh through the Word. Where we have unbridled lust, there is no discipline being put upon our flesh. Whatever our flesh feels like doing it sends a signal to our brain, which at that point we have to make a decision, am I going to do this or not? If we have no morals, no standards and if Christ is not our all or our source for everything, then we are not going to make an attempt to discipline ourselves – our fleshly desires that contradict God's Word.

So as Christians it is not that we are perfect when Christ comes inside of us, because we are not – we are just babes. And there are a lot of inabilities in our lives yet, but truth and grace are within us to help build a strong foundation.

Remember the parable of the sower. The enemy has sowed things in our lives years ago to trip us up today, and he will play those cards in our lives at the right time. So, grace within the foundation is a hedge that is around us and that hedge will keep us protected, just as parents do for their small child. They run moving things out of the way so their child does not hit it, or hurt themselves. That is what grace does, it moves the devil out of the way because we are not ready to deal with those things in our lives yet.

God Drops the Hedge

But there is a time when God, within the foundation, drops the hedge and lets the enemy go after things in our lives that are hindering our walk. Things that we do not even know are there inside of us. When that happens, we see a part of ourselves that we have not seen since we were born again or baptized with the Holy Ghost! We thought that we were long past these stumbling blocks only to find they are still very much a part of our lives. So, the grace that once had our back and was protecting us had been lifted, but it was lifted only when He was ready to extract that ugliness out of our lives. For it must be extracted or it will eat its way into the foundation of our lives, and tear down everything that we have been able to successfully build in our lives. I am speaking about what has been spiritually built, and what has been built into our character – how it has been formed into His likeness.

Just like any thief, the key is to first get into the house. And once the thief gets into the house, he still has to unlock the doors that are locked. There is a reason Christ Our Lord gives us the keys of the Kingdom, for there are different departments and areas in our lives and in our souls, where the Lord is still protecting us, while He is building us up in another area.

In the day that we live in, today, we are going to find out who is all talk and who has a strong foundation as Christians. If we have a strong foundation, we will not be easily deceived. One of the biggest problems in today's Christian society, or the world for that matter, is deception. The more mixture we have in our lives, the more susceptible we will be to deception.

Even though we may be limited in Godly character, Christ

our Lord the Chief Corner Stone is purging and giving life to our foundation. He wants to constantly strengthen us with Godly character – love, joy, peace, long suffering, gentleness, goodness, faith, temperance – those things that are immovable, and impregnable.

The Bible says tribulation worketh patience and patience experience (Romans 5:3-4). If we are not constantly moving through the process of tribulation and graduating and being delivered, and going forth from it, we will never have experience. How can we counsel anybody else in what to do, or how to go through trials of affliction, and how to stand that place of refining, if we ourselves have not experienced it?

Parable of the Two Houses

If we are not moving forward in the Lord, He already knows this about our lives, but so does the enemy. Christ Our Lord talks about this in the parable of the two houses. We tend to look at people on the outside and think their house looks good. Just like when Samuel went and saw Jesse's first born son Eliab and thought that he looked good – surely the anointing is upon Him. But God said, *"No I have rejected him,"* and the Lord goes on to say the same thing about each one of his sons until he comes to David. The Lord did not tell Samuel which one it was, He kept telling him which one it was not! God's ways are not like our ways.

So, when we look at the two houses, they can both look alike on the outside. But then comes the storms and the winds come and we find out they are not both the same. Christ our Lord emphasized there was something different about each house – the foundation. God is attempting to free His children of the mixture that is in their foundation, because of the deception that is arising in the earth. Remember, what we believe is a part of our foundation and it will either make our foundation secure or unstable.

When it comes to our foundations, we are not going to do what we are saying, we are going to do what we believe. Many, in the Church today, say one thing but do something different. And most, unless the opportunity presents itself, do not know what they believe. This is the main reason the Father allows storms into our lives, because we will not know what we believe until this is done. If we know anything about spiritual things, there is one thing we should understand: the devil makes tests, God makes tests and we make tests. We make tests when we try to take things into our own hands. Peter says that we bring things upon ourselves and God is going to make sure we learn from it.

Controlled Burns

God will allow one test after another to come into our lives, when we insist on doing things our way. And when He does, He will just simply stop protecting us from our own flesh, causing us to be drawn away in our own lust and enticed. Because tests are the standard way of the Christian life, but tests designed to hurt you is not, that only happens when we want our own way. When it is normal test and trials that he allows this is the wonderful thing about what God does! I call them controlled burns, because what the devil brings on the scene is not controlled burns. It is like firemen in training, when they go to put out fires there are backup fire trucks ready to go if things get out of control, or if things get beyond their capabilities.

In the same way, we have the angels of the Lord who stand and watch over us, while we are being tested, who are instructed not to allow the demons to do things to us that we are not ready to handle. God watches over us, as the fiery darts of hell come against us, trying to bring our entire house down. God will always give us the spiritual drills that we need to help prepare us for the war that comes to rage against us. And that war is mostly internal and not external.

Then we have the other house and the same storm and wind beats against it, and boom it comes tumbling down. Now which one would you have put your money on? Because they both look the same – how would you know which one would stand or fall? I submit to you, that's the way it is in the Church.

A Storm is Coming

Many people in the Church are like the fallen house. And believe me brothers and sisters, a storm is coming. A storm of such magnitude, such level of darkness, it is going to crush many in the Church, but it will not be unto righteousness. It will be a direct attack against our spiritual character – the fruit of the spirit. There will be many who will begin to rise up within the Church to do us harm. And, yes, the attacks will be within the house of God. David said that his wounds came from within the house of the Lord. It is in the house of the Lord where our guards are let down, we do not walk around in the house of the Lord with our shields up.

A civil war is about to happen in the Body of Christ and we must maintain Godly character. The weapons of our warfare are not carnal, we do not fight each other with our tongue. It will be our tongue – this one member that will cause us to be disqualified from moving on and finishing the building of our house. We will be hit with the direct attacks against our spiritual character. We are going to have to learn to turn the other cheek: to walk in unoffended love. We are going to have to learn how to pray for those who despitefully use us. If we have been growing in Christ and allowing the Holy Spirit to purify our soul and strengthen our foundation, we will make it. Turning the other cheek, walking in love, holding our tongue, not criticizing, not holding grudges, not dogging people; but many in the Body of Christ have not practiced this in their walk. Resisting these things are the very things that strengthen our foundation, that will enable us to ensure that we will stand in the evil day.

The evil day is here and we have come to the point where Paul says, after you have done all to stand, stand. Here is where we are now, we are on the last stand, the last one. It is during this time that He will trim away all of the fat, all of the excess that is in our lives. All those things that has kept Him from bringing us into a rich place. A place of elevation – a place of exaltation.

Now that we are at this point, the enemy is not going to just give up. He will try to get us to cast away our confidence, and if he is successful then everything that God has done on the inside of us will have been all for nothing. The last thing we need to listen to is the world and what they are broadcasting!

Everything Will be Recompensed!

But if we do not grow weary in doing good and faint not, then we can be assured everything that we have suffered through, everything that we have lost, everything that we have went through; the hard times, the tears, the sorrow will all be recompensed! It is with patience that we get back what was stolen from us. We must wait for it – it will come and not tarry!

When the enemy has been allowed to successfully engage you, or have access to an area of your life, remember that while that is happening that God is not mad at you! He is trying to recover, redeem and restore all things in your life and make you better for it, and suffering is a part of that recovery process. So, I encourage you, fall on the Rock and let Him have what He is after in your life! Better to fall upon the Rock and be broken to pieces, than for the Rock to fall upon you and crush you altogether!

The Eye of the Storm

Remember, the weapons of our warfare are not carnal, nor can we run away from the storms. Instead, we are in the eye of the storm. The eye moves with us until we take a stand. The Lord already knows who will win – who will succeed, and because of that fact He went ahead of us and placed certain things into our lives to help us. He already knows who will succumb to Him, who will say yes to Him, and who will surrender all to Him.

This is why we have all that we need to build a firm foundation. For deep within the mysteries of Christ Our Lord's' Words, we have everything that we need.

* * *

Chapter 1 : Blessed Are The Poor In Spirit

The Old Testament contains the Ten Commandments which governs the conduct of the children of Israel and how they were to live through the wilderness. Of course, it speaks not to just life in the wilderness, but how to govern their lives as they walked with Him for the rest of their days.

As New Testament saints we are given the Ten Beatitudes. In them, Christ our Lord is expounding more on the Ten Commandments; thereby, giving us the Sermon on the Mount to guide our earthly pilgrimage. Just as the law was given on Mount Sanai, so were the Beatitudes – the inward law, given on a mountain in Capernaum.

Core Message of the Lord

The teachings on the Sermon on the Mount were the core message of the Lord for the believers. They were the building blocks to secure a firm foundation in one's life. They are the essence of what it is to be a Christian and follower of Christ. We should meditate deeply on these verses and everything our Lord taught so that we can become transformed into His likeness.

Every one of the Beatitudes are preceded by the word "blessed." Although this word is sometimes translated as "happy" especially in the Old Testament, it means to have a joy and peace that God alone can give. The word "blessed" then involves a partaking of the joy, peace, serenity and state of bliss enjoyed in heaven. So, the Lord is saying, I bring to you heaven on earth. I want to teach you how-to live on earth just like you would live in heaven. This is what He is saying in His teaching of the Beatitudes. Because happiness comes from the root word "hap" or "happenchance" which means something that happens to you by luck or good fortune, that immediately tells us that we should not be dependent upon our circumstances, right? For this reason, "happy" is not a good translation.

God's joy and state of blessedness is not dependent upon circumstances, situations or people. God is the source of our joy; it is the fruit of the Spirit. As we seek to live by these Beatitudes and have them work out in us their eternal purpose for our lives, we will experience the joy of heaven upon the earth.

Psalm 16:11

Thou wilt shew me the path of life: in thy presence is fulness of joy; at thy right hand there are pleasures for evermore.

Let us look at the first one, briefly, not in depth.

Matthew 5:3

Blessed are the poor in spirit for theirs is the kingdom of heaven.

What Does it Mean to be Poor in Spirit?

Have you ever meditated on and thought about what it really means to be poor in spirit? Being poor in spirit from the Lord's perspective means that we recognize our own unworthiness and inability. This is the first prerequisite to receive anything from God. It is why He put this one first.

The Beatitudes are well illustrated by the testimony of the Lord, concerning His own dependence on His Father.

John 5:19

The Son can do nothing of Himself but what He seeth what the Father do.

Christ our Lord exemplified this in everything that He did and spoke, He is the only One to follow.

So being poor in spirit signifies that we recognize our total dependency on the Lord. Now brothers and sisters, you know as well as I do that these things do not come to us automatically. We run across Christians all the time that do not have the character of Christ formed within their souls. This is what will make us successful as a people on the earth. When I say people, I mean as the Body of Christ. The things that appear to make us the weakest from man's perspective actually make us the strongest on the earth from God's perspective. But, again, it is an attitude of worship. We have to change our mindset. We have to change our perspective in how we live our lives, that we may learn the Fathers ways.

Attitude of a Beggar

Basically, it is an attitude – a heart posture of a beggar, but we cannot abase ourselves any more than that. That is the attitude of the Father Himself; that is the attitude of the Christ our Lord. I have nothing and I can do nothing without My Father. We have to build our lives on this mindset.

Matthew 11:29
Take my yoke upon you, and learn of me; for I am meek and lowly in heart: and ye shall find rest unto your souls.

If the Lord perceives Himself this way as lowly and abased, then we must certainly have the same mentality.

This beautiful attitude was displayed in the story with the Phoenician woman. When the Lord said to her that it was not fit for Him to give the children's bread to dogs. Right there a lot of us would have gotten upset – taken an offense, and would have stopped following the Lord, causing many to be lost and burning in hell because the Lord called them a dog.

But look at this woman's humble response in Mark 7:28, "Yes, Lord. Yet the dogs under the table eat of the children's crumbs." That is amazing! And because of her humility and her perception of her lowliness, she got what she wanted from the Lord. There were many that did not in that day. There were many that could not even get that close to Him. What set her apart was how she saw herself.

A True Beggar is Grateful

In other words, she was begging for the Lord to help her. She did not demand the best part of that meal for herself. She was content to receive the crumbs that fell on the floor. So, a true beggar is grateful for every little morsel they can get. At large, as Christians, we are some very ungrateful people. Especially, us westerners. I have been all over the world and many think that westerners are some of the most ungrateful and arrogant people. This must change, if we want to fulfill our Kingdom purpose on earth.

This quality of being poor in spirit, which is total dependency upon the Lord, is developed through severe trials. This is why we do not see it in very many people who are walking on this road. We must become broken before Him; this is what our trials do. They take us beyond the limits of our own capabilities – our strength and wisdom, that we might learn to depend on the Lord's strength and wisdom. That is why it is the poor in spirit who will receive the Kingdom of heaven.

The Shaping of our Souls

Notice, He did not say it is those who will make it to heaven – but those who will receive the Kingdom. Let us put it this way. What makes heaven is God. We enter in through Him, then we have access to everywhere and everything that is inside of Him. It is not automatic for every believer to have access to every place in heaven. Why? Because very few are willing to sit on the Master Potter's wheel and allow the Lord to shape their souls like clay in His hands, until every foreign particle has been removed. Until every wrinkle has been smoothed; thereby; purifying their soul constantly by adding water to it, which typifies the washing of the Word to make their soul more compatible with His character.

The more God can break us under His hand, the more He can trust us with, and the more we move closer to Him in a more intimate relationship. We will progress from believer to servant, from servant to friend, from friend to son and from son to bride. An attitude of worship means this must be forever before us. We must meditate on these things, for it is the poor in spirit who will have every access, provision and protection that can be found in Him alone, enabling them to complete the works the Father has sent them to this earth to complete.

* * *

Chapter 2: Blessed Are They That Mourn

God endeavors to build a foundation in your life to ensure the purpose for which He has called you – to become like Him, so that you may finish your destiny. If you are going to build a 12-story building, you cannot put the same foundation in place that you would use for a four-story building. The higher up you go, the deeper the foundation must be laid. Some who have been going through so much hell – many difficulties, are asking, "When will I come out of this wilderness?" But a positive way to look at it instead is to ask, "Why is the devil so afraid of my purpose?" The devil knows more about you than you do yourself. And if he can keep you from your purpose, you become a lesser threat to him. Remember, to suffer is to mourn; thereby, producing in you a far more exceeding internal weight of glory.

Caring for Others

To be effective in the Kingdom we must have a holy mourning for our own sins and for the state of the unsaved, and for the state of the Church in general, including backslidden believers. In scripture there are basically two kinds of mourning. There are more, but these are the two principal ones.

1. Mourning because of one's own shortcoming or sinful ways. That is the deep within you calling unto the deep in Him.
2. Mourning because of the state of a loved one, the Church, or a nation. This kind of mourning will stir up the spirit of intercession within your soul.

The first aspect of mourning is when we fall short of the glory of God, which we all have done. When we are weak in a certain area and we yield to temptation, part of the process of repentance and restoration includes mourning. Not self-pity, that is a counterfeit of true mourning. Paul speaks to the Corinthians about a believer who had fallen into sin and was then restored.

2 Corinthians 7:9-11,13

Now I rejoice, not that ye were made sorry, but that ye sorrowed to repentance: for ye were made sorry after a godly manner, that ye might receive damage by us in nothing.10 For godly sorrow worketh repentance to salvation not to be repented of: but the sorrow of the world worketh death.11

8

For behold this selfsame thing, that ye sorrowed after a godly sort, what carefulness it wrought in you, yea, what clearing of yourselves, yea, what indignation, yea, what fear, yea, what vehement desire, yea, what zeal, yea, what revenge! In all things ye have approved yourselves to be clear in this matter. **13** Therefore we were comforted in your comfort: yea, and exceedingly the more joyed we for the joy of Titus, because his spirit was refreshed by you all.

Paul had to send a reprimand to this man. The result of dealing with sin head-on was that this man repented. He mourns with great sorrow because of his sin. The result was repentance, restoration and comfort. Remember, Christ Our Lord said, *"Blessed are they that mourn for they shall be comforted."* Then you have the mourning that comes upon God's people when an individual, a nation or the Church is backslidden. In the days of the prophet Ezekiel, the angel of the Lord was sent through Jerusalem to put a mark upon the foreheads of those godly saints who mourned and cried for the wickedness of the city.

Ezekiel 9:4

And the Lord said unto him, Go through the midst of the city, through the midst of Jerusalem, and set a mark upon the foreheads of the men that sigh and that cry for all the abominations that be done in the midst thereof.

The Lord promised to spare these "holy mourners" when the Babylonian's destroyed Jerusalem. We desperately need these types of mourners to rise up in North America. The promise to those who mourn, either in a godly way for their own sins or for the backslidden condition of others, is that they will be comforted.

2 Corinthians 1:3

Blessed be God, even the Father of our Lord Jesus Christ, the Father of mercies, and the God of all comfort;

Let us look even deeper into this mystery of how this mourning takes place in us, and how the Father uses it to rid us of the tares and weaknesses that the enemy uses to try to destroy us.

Are We Doing What the Father is Asking?

The scriptures call the Lord the Master Builder. He is the Chief Cornerstone. So, for Him to successfully allow us to be built on His foundation, He must make sure that it is laid properly. There are many in the Body that do not have a proper foundation. They are doing things for God, seemingly good things that He did not initiate; therefore, He cannot bless what they are doing. Though some may be blessed by what we do, what will it really profit us if we become a castaway? Each one of us will have to stand before the Lord on that Day not for the purpose of judgment of sin, but for the judgment of reward. We will be judged on whether or not we had done what the Father asked us to do. In that moment of reckoning, a fire will come out of the presence of the Lord and it will burn

10

up everything in our lives that He did not initiate. It will not matter how good it may have been!

1 Corinthians 3:15

If any man's work shall be burned, he shall suffer loss: but he himself shall be saved; yet so as by fire.

If the Lord did not initiate it and it is not of the Spirit but of the flesh, it will profit nothing. It will not matter how good it was or what it accomplished. If it is flesh, then it is an enemy to God and it is keeping us from God's purpose for our lives. In other words, we have made ourselves our own god.

Brothers and Sisters, we are in the last part of the last days. The finish line is in view and we must make sure all distractions are out of our lives. Everyone knows the story of the tortoise and the hare, or the cartoon with the rabbit and turtle. The rabbit had fun knowing he had the speed, thinking he had time to waste. But the turtle was focused, and while the rabbit was in his pursuit of fun, the turtle never took his eyes off the finish line. He kept the same pace and not only finished, but won!

1 Corinthians 9:24

Know ye not that they which run in a race run all, but one receiveth the prize? So run, that ye may obtain.

We can be rest assured that the enemy is going to throw all sorts of distractions into our lives. And some of those distractions are going to be religious distractions; they look good, feel good, sound good but it is not of God. If it is not of God, it is then fleshly and our flesh will profit us nothing. We need to make

11

sure and examine everything in our lives through the eyes of the Holy Spirit and that we are building with the right things – the right Kingdom materials. For only then will He allow us to move into our destiny, when our foundation is secure in His ways.

Sacrificing our Lives

In the story where Christ our Lord spoke about the two houses, one built his house on the rock and the other on sand. In one sense, God is building internally within our soul, by breaking and crushing us, bringing difficulties into our lives so that everything that is not of Him can be laid wasted. When that happens, we are building a firm foundation, because we are sacrificing our very lives. The foundation is the character of Christ being laid in us. So that means that God has predetermined every situation and circumstance in our lives. They have all been orchestrated by heaven and not hell, if we do not allow it.

The Lord will allow the enemy to contest every godly decision we make, so says the sower. But we are dealing with a God Who knows the end from the beginning. Why is this so important? Because we are in transition and for us to move on our foundation must be solid. Not only to go on, but to survive the days ahead. The closer we get to the Lord the easier it is for us to fall, because the flesh is always with us. And the flesh will always try to take credit for what God is doing. That is why it is so important that our lives have been crushed and broken by the Lord before we move on in Him. Being a doer of the word will lawfully attract the enemy into your life. He has a right to test everything you claim to stand upon when it comes to truth.

Mark 4:15

And these are they by the wayside, where the word is sown; but when they have heard, Satan cometh immediately, and taketh away the word that was sown in their hearts.

There were many in the 40's and 50's who moved on in ministry but were crushed by the enemy, not by the Lord. The Lord was not able to bring them under His hand and break them. I do not care how much we may know and how wonderful we may think we are or how spiritual we are, we all need to be broken by the Potter. All of us have things interwoven into our lives that need to be extracted and the only way for it to be extracted is for us to be broken.

Luke 20:17-18

And he beheld them, and said, What is this then that is written, The stone which the builders rejected, the same is become the head of the corner? **18** Whosoever shall fall upon that stone shall be broken; but on whomsoever it shall fall, it will grind him to powder.

This is what the Lord is endeavoring to do and there is always a time factor to His plans for us. So, if we get serious, so too will the Lord. The Lord endeavors to put a people on display now and He will do it, even knowing that down the road we will stumble and fall and be a detriment to ourselves and ultimately become an enemy to the Cross. That is what happened to Judas.

The Inward Life

Christ our Lord takes a good look at the inward life, so that He can ensure that as He pours Himself upon us, the more we will humble ourselves. The closer we get to Him and to our destiny, the more trouble we are in if our soul is not anchored. Yet, we must have the mindset not to be interested in going three quarters of the way, only to fall back. That means our prayer to the Lord should be, "Judge me. Show me my wrongdoings and what I need to do to be right with You Lord and right with man." We must be willing to do whatever we have to do, so that we do not fail.

It is time now brothers and sisters to start putting the spotlight on the little things in our lives. It is the little foxes that will destroy God's plans. This is what the enemy is zeroing in on now. Things that we have so precariously ignored in our lives for such a long time. How do we do that? We have to use what the Lord gave us; it is what I call the sifter. The battle for our mind is intensifying because the Lord is putting the finishing touches on His Body.

And while doing so, He is trying to ensure that we transition safely with all of our armor in place. The character building that has been going on in our lives, takes its toll and impacts the armor that we wear. The enemy is endeavoring to slip in under the wire into our lives, so we must scrutinize the littlest of things in our lives, now! Paul speaks of the sifter in Philippians 4:8, when he says, "Whatever things are true." Here I can apply the sifter as one who sifts flour and removes all of the things that will defile my freshly made bread. The enemy hides himself within the thoughts of our mind so it is of the utmost importance for what we allow to drop inside of us. So, whatever things are true. This is the first thing that we must do and ensure that those things that are coming into our lives – into our ears, that they are truth. If they are not, then we must stop them immediately because if those things get down inside of us, they will erode our foundation.

Things that took years to destabilize us or strengthen us, only take days now. That is both positive and negative. Whatsoever things are lovely. We interact throughout the day hearing things, seeing things, talking about things, yet is it truth, is it lovely? We have to apply the sifter and stop it from going inside of us if it is not. Whatsoever things are honest. If it is not honest, we need to stop it immediately. Whatsoever things are of good report. Is it a good report what we are hearing or speaking? Do those words bring a blessing or curse? If there be any virtue coming to you, if there be any praise coming to you, think on these things. Let me interject this lest you misunderstand what I'm saying, the praise as you offer it to God, and it drops inside of you is to keep the seed watered within you which is part of the joy of the Lord. The attack of the mind is intensifying and is not business as usual. We cannot go on with life as usual. We must scrutinize everything, because the enemy will wrap words that are cursed within words that are truth. It can be truth and not lovely, lovely and not honest, so we must stand watch.

15

Must be a Student of the Word

As a young Christian in the Lord, I taught myself that whatever I hear, including people preaching, to immediately ask myself what did the Word say about what I was hearing. We must be a student of the Word. When we give ourselves to the Word, we might not necessarily have read a particular thing in the Word but then the Holy Spirit becomes wisdom to us because he is on the inside of us.

For example, if Christ our Lord is made unto you wisdom and I am three years old spiritually, and you are thirteen years old spiritually then wisdom will rise up in me as a three-year-old. And I will see something I did not see before as a three-year-old, but on a three-year-old level. But by the grace of God based upon our need at the moment and the urgency in our lives, then God will release a thirteen-year-old's wisdom into our spiritual age of three because God is good.

At this point, in Church history, we are crossing over regardless of our spiritual age for grace is doing what we could not do. As a three-year-old spiritually in transition and a thirteen-year-old in transition, both of them are walking in grace and wisdom, appearing to be the same age because of what the Lord is doing now. The initiative that He is taking now is based upon our doing our part. We need to be asking the Holy Spirit to shine the Light upon us and reveal the errors within us. Some things we may be capable of accomplishing may be something that God has been trying to get us to do, but we have not done so because certain things have not been released within us, yet.

The potential is there because we have allowed ourselves

to be broken. We have been willing to go through the fiery furnace of affliction. But there can still be certain things in the natural – carnal things, that we do not want to let go of and God requires it of us. For He cannot release within us what is necessary to deal with that vulnerability within us, because character is forged through fire. And if God gives something that is not built on the inside of us, the likelihood of us losing it is very big.

Character Forged in the Fire

When the Lord pours out His glory on one whose character has not been forged in the fire; thereby, producing humility, they will take credit for what God is doing and will be resisted by God. This is why the Lord has withheld pouring His glory into us, because we must be filled with Him first, meaning like Him in character. If not, we will in turn get filled with ourselves – pride, and it will be to our destruction. That is why the closer we get to Him; the quicker we can fall. This is why after every big blessing in our lives will be our greatest chance of falling. This is why the Lord spends so much time breaking us, pulling us out of trusting in ourselves. This is why He withholds certain things from us

Paul declares In Galatians 2:20, "I am crucified with Christ." Now this does not sound like the same Paul in Romans 7 does it? "When I would to do good, evil is present. Oh, wretched man that I am, who will deliver me from the body of this death?" Our flesh profits us nothing, and when the Bible speaks of the flesh life it is not talking about a piece of meat. It is talking about our total existence before Christ our Lord came inside of us. Our flesh has a life and out of the flesh we live, we move, we have our existence. Everything is in our flesh life thanks to Adam. The power that is in our soul is pushed into our flesh life.

In Galatians 2, Paul describes this process. This process should have been happening in all of us for quite some time. He cries out in chapter seven and eight, "I cannot do anything with my flesh, when I want to do good evil is here." How is evil getting access? Through the flesh life, for it has its own life and it is an enemy to God. We cannot offer God anything from our flesh. If we do, it will not be accepted. We have many people prophesying in the flesh, preaching in the flesh, leading worship in the flesh all thinking God is accepting it. Remember, God is the only One Who can divide the soul from the spirit, and we see the Apostle Paul struggling with this. The Lord told Paul that he would be shown what great things that he must suffer, for His name's sake. Many in the Body of Christ think that only applies to Paul or to preachers, but it applies to all believers. God has predetermined a level of suffering to come into our lives, according to our purpose and what is in our soul that needs uprooted, that we may become like Him.

We get a glimpse of the Apostle Paul and what he had to overcome. He was stoned, left for dead two or three times, shipwrecked, with his own brethren wanting to kill him. He was constantly running for his life. If Paul were alive today, most Christians would say that he was not in the will of God. That is because most Christians do not understand God's redemptive purposes for our suffering; therefore, they look at the wrong thing thinking they are in the will of God if all is going well in their lives. Listen, dear people of God, if you are not having difficulty in your life then the devil has already got you!

Crucified with Christ

Our dear brother Paul gets to the end of his life and he says, "I am crucified with Christ." What does that mean? It means that I am living my purpose. I am walking in obedience. I am doing what I was created to do. And most importantly, it means I am becoming like Him because I am crucified unto what I was created to do and become. We cannot become like Him if we are not crucified with Him. It is explicitly designed by God to pull out of us everything that is an enemy against Him. At the same time, He has a timetable that these things should have been out of our lives

Paul says I am crucified. He is saying, I have been broken, I have been crushed by Him but nevertheless I live. I am not dead although there were many times that this crucifixion, this suffering could have killed me, but I lived. Yet not I, but Christ is living or has been manifested in me. This is the same test the first Adam failed too. So, we must decide, will we have His life or our own soul life? Our life on earth is not about making it to heaven. It is about how much of our life or His life that we will have when we get there. We cannot do whatever we want with our lives for He bought us with His blood; therefore, He owns us. If we have been bought with a price, the question is will we pay the same price that He paid? We will not love our own life, unto death? A death where we will exchange our will for His will.

19

That means we cannot be what we want to be anymore. We cannot marry who we may want to marry. If our lives have already been predetermined, how can we do what we want to do? If there is a book in heaven that is filled with a record of what our lives are to be like, that means our lives on earth must match what is in that book. It is one of the books that will be opened when we stand to be judged on that day. Not judged unto sin, but judged unto rewards. This is why such a struggle happened in the Apostle Paul's life. Christ must be formed or grow in us; it is not automatic. He came into us as a Seed. We need to ask ourselves where is He now in us – are we a baby, a child or a son?

As Christ our Lord is formed within us, we yield our members to Him that He may do His work through us because of the purpose of training and adaptability that is stirring us in the right direction, as He gives us instructions. And because we have very little of Him on the inside of us, it becomes a process where our spirit man grows and matures. Then we take off with the best of our abilities but the help that He gives will come through the anointing He has for each of us. It will help us to conform to the anointing that is within us that we can complete the eternal purpose for our lives. This is the life of becoming One with Him. We do not know where Christ begins or ends because we are becoming One with Him. In other words, everything that is passing through our spirit from a revelatory standpoint is attempting to be engrafted into our soul, where the real us is being built that He may reside.

This is what Paul is saying. The life I now live in the flesh, I live by the faith of the Son of God – I and the Son have become One. What He thinks, I know what He thinks, when He feels, I know what He feels. He does not come to visit me; He dwells within me all the time – He is abiding in me. Paul experienced a life of habitation with Christ, not a visitation. Adam had the visitation, the next step was supposed to be habitation, but he never got there.

The Life of Christ is Birthed through Suffering

So, this is the war between the first Adam and the second Adam. The first Adam was earthy, the second Adam was of the Spirit, and that is the life that we should be after the life of Christ. But it is only birthed through suffering. Even if we have pain in our bodies now; physical pain, let God make it redemptive. That physical pain can bring us into the fellowship of His suffering, and it will produce the life of Christ within us, if we do what Paul tells us to do.

2 Corinthians 4:17-18

For our light affliction, which is but for a moment, worketh for us a far more exceeding and eternal weight of glory; **18** While we look not at the things which are seen, but at the things which are not seen: for the things which are seen are temporal; but the things which are not seen are eternal.

If we are not looking at the things that are seen, then we are not looking at what we feel either. Notice verse 17 where he says these light afflictions are for a moment. Here is a man that had been stoned three times and left for dead. Paul knew what it felt like to be without food, while running for his life. Yet, everywhere he went, he either started a revival or a riot and called it all light afflictions! If that were us today, we would be wanting a big trophy. But Paul knew all his afflictions were working a more exceedingly eternal weight of glory, and the same is true for us, if we do not look at the things that are seen.

We Need to Stop Whining

We need to stop whining about the trials that we are going through. We need to stop whining about what people are saying and doing and how they are treating us. We need to stop whining about what the devil is doing. The devil is the devil, and he has a lot of two legged friends. We need to stop whining and start letting it work for our good. In everything we are to give thanks, while we are going through our afflictions. The devil cannot stand praises, nor can he stand to be around true praise, so we need to put him to flight with our praise and thanksgiving.

I know this is difficult when the Lord is crushing our soul where He is after an event in our lives that impacted our soul for so long and is still controlling our lives, such as unforgiveness or strife. It is just like a blister that we want to burst open. That when we do, everything that has formulated within it comes oozing out. That is like our pain – that is what God is after – to extract that out of our soul that we may be healed, and mature and grow into His purpose for our lives. That thing that has shaped our lives and has caused us to negatively act the way we do, talk the way we talk, think the way we think, will cause us to come to a place where we cry out for God to take that thing out of us. Well, we need to realize that is what

He is trying to do, but it is going to take the Cross. That means we have to be willing to do it His way, not our way anymore.

The Knife of the Holy Spirit

This thing that sticks to you like silly putty that you have been trying to get rid of is like spitting in the wind. We know what happens when we spit in the wind, right? This is why Paul was able to say no more. It is why he allowed himself to come under the knife of the Holy Spirit. So, when these events keep coming back and increasing, we have to deal with our lack of spirituality because the devil will quickly make us think we are worse off than we really are. He will try to make us think that we are not progressing spiritually. And he will make us think that we thought that we had gotten rid of this problem a long time ago and this is why God does not like us, or is angry with us. I call it the Job factor. The same game that he played with job, the devil will try with us and it becomes even more difficult to overcome.

We need to understand it is God dropping the hedge and that He is after the tares that are within our soul. And if we can maintain, apply the filter, get on our knees and cry out to God and pray we will live and not die. God is trying to do what we want Him to do, if He can, and once that tear is removed it is replaced with glory. What has been standing between us and Him is removed. This purification process determines how much we really love Him. It determines our humility by how much we are willing to lay our pride at the feet of Christ Our Lord. Passing or failing this test will determine it.

Job's Life

We cannot do this ourselves and the last person we need resisting us is God. When we look at Jobs' life, in the natural does it look like God loved him? None of his friends thought God loved him. This guy is sitting with boils all over him and scraping them off. He stinks to the high heavens and has lost everything. Some of us would have backslid after losing the first house, let alone three or four houses. Some of us would have backslid when we lost our kids. He never did, even when his wife turned against him – the very one that should have been standing with him. The devil will always have someone to use to try to cripple us emotionally, and especially when he thinks we are down for the count!

Job lost his houses, he lost his children, he lost everything. His body is not working right and on top of it all, the very one that is closest to him – his wife, one who should comfort him, tells him to curse God and die. He put up a good fight, at first. He had enough life left in him to say you are a foolish woman. Naked I came into this world, naked I will go out. But then he started whining. But we have to give Job a lot of credit, God did. Job did not have what we have today, he did not have Christ in him, he did not have the Word. Job did not have any of the things that we have, but he made it through. My point is when we read this story it does not appear that God loved him, and at times this is how Paul felt but it is also how he got to be where he was in Christ.

Brothers and Sisters, this is how the life of Christ is manifest in us and crushes the flesh life. But while we are going through all that, the flesh life is screaming and screaming and the only thing we can do with the flesh life is train it like we do a dog. We have to be repetitive, exercise it to discern good and evil. We have to say you have to do this flesh! You have to do that now! And we have to make sure we do it during the Job factor of our lives. Constantly applying the filter, bringing it under, falling on the rock, all the while crying out to God will train our flesh while walking out most difficult times.

Understanding Heaven's Ways

But be encouraged, for every time we have a victory it gets easier and easier. And our flesh will start discerning evil, but there is that period where it is the most difficult, it is hard. But we have to keep thinking what is on the other side? More of Him! Can we see now in all these situations how we cannot stand before Him and tell Him we loved Him, when He watched us take the flesh life instead of the Spirit life. When all of the angels watched us take the flesh life, instead of His life. Each test, each battle is playing out every day and the more we overcome, the more we get through a battle, the easier it is to crush the flesh life and the more we are purified. And the more His love grows inside of us because we are loving Him through it all. We can now love others with that same love. We can now have pity on other people who are having difficulties too, we will not judge because of what we have been through.

We have to understand this is heaven's way. This is the gospel that Christ our Lord and the apostles preached, but most of the Church either do not know it, or they do not want to know it; therefore, refusing it. There is a false grace floating around in the Body of Christ that says it has all been finished on the Cross so we do not have to suffer, that Christ has suffered it all for us. That is a half-truth. That is like me giving you half of a coin and I do not give you the other half. A half-truth presented wrongly becomes a lie, the way Lucifer presented himself to Eve in the Garden, and to the Lord during His time of testing.

In the Garden, Lucifer told Eve she would be as God knowing good and evil. When we omit the last three words – good and evil, we will understand it better. Eve believed that she would know good and evil like God. Eve's struggle was that she did not know as much as Adam, but that was God's order for the family and it was Adam's job to teach his wife. So the serpent used that shortcoming against her, and she failed her test. With the Lord, Lucifer quoted scripture to Him out of context, thereby, giving Him a half-truth. Therefore, you must work out your own salvation with fear and trembling.

Make It Redemptive

So, what can we see that the Lord has been endeavoring to do within us? He is building a firm foundation. So, I am saying to you, whatever pain is in your life, even if it is physical, make it redemptive now. Within you, your spirit mourns for Him. This is what helps you to surrender to the breaking of your soul, because on the other side of the breaking is more of Him. Even if it is the result of your carnality, your stupidity, your sins, your disobedience, or whatever it may be. Make it redemptive by allowing the Holy Spirit to uproot the tares in your soul by purifying and transforming your soul into His image and likeness, in your words, thoughts and deeds. Stop letting the enemy condemn you, instead walk in the Spirit. Know God is turning it for your good. Know he knows how to get something good out of your worst sin or trauma. Know It is working for you – not against you, Hallelujah!

* * *

Chapter 3: Humility

The Bible looks at our lives from two perspectives; when we build a house and lay its foundation or how a seed is planted and it takes root and grows. The principle is the same when it comes to the process of our developing or growing up. Christ Our Lord said, *"That except a grain of wheat falls into the ground and dies, it abides alone."* What is He saying? That when Christ's Seed goes inside of us, then we must deny ourselves, the flesh life, if we are to bear abundant, everlasting good fruit. And through obedience that Seed begins to unveil our purpose and destiny. As the root begins to develop and take hold of our souls, we will have a firm foundation laid that will enable us to survive the storm of life.

Seeds within our Souls

In contrast, the sower talks about the four categories of ground that we can have inside our souls. It is possible to have all four at one time. It depends on what we believe and how obedient we are to His Word and His ways. For example; some people are obedient to God when it comes to tithes and offerings, but disobedient when it comes to forsaking not the assembling of the saints. Some are obedient to God when it comes to walking in love and turning the other cheek, while others are not obedient when it comes to forgiving and holding grudges. We can have a strong foundation – or a good root, in one area and lacking in another.

Many of those foundations will become eroded causing the roots to be uprooted by the dark storms on the horizon. We are seeing racial tension increase in our nation. Only spiritual warfare is going to help the situation. When we see this racial tension, we have to determine whether or not our response is coming from the God kind of love, or racism.

Matthew 5:5-6

Blessed are the meek; for they shall inherit the earth. Blessed are they which do hunger and thirst after righteousness: for they shall be filled.

We can do things that can destroy the hunger for doing right on the inside of us. Without hunger we destroy our desire to draw near to the Lord. When we recognize this taking place in our lives, whether from the weight of sin or from distractions, we need to stop whatever it is.

To hunger and thirst after righteousness is another way of saying to be filled with doing what is right. Blessed are the merciful for they will show mercy. Depending upon which spirit we yield to will determine if we become better or bitter. When we suffer certain things, it can become very easy to show mercy.

Blessed are the peacemakers for they will be called the Sons of God. When we have been purified, and have learned how to be merciful when going through hard times, we come through with that same attitude and bring peace to others.

Different Levels of Persecution

Blessed are those who are persecuted for righteousness' sake. We want to make sure that we are in the process of bringing forth righteousness in our lives when the persecution comes, for then it will come with a promise. For theirs is the Kingdom of heaven. Only godly persecution and suffering brings us into oneness with Him. There are different levels of persecution. If we are a child of God and born again, there is a level of persecution that comes against that truth. If we are a child of God born again and filled with the Holy Spirit, there is a level of persecution that comes against that truth. If we are a child of God, born of the Spirit and walking in righteousness with our love for God growing, there is a level of persecution that comes against that truth. If we are a child of God who has purposed to walk in our destiny and calling, there is a level of persecution that comes against that truth.

There are people who come against us on our jobs. Some

may or may not know that we are righteous. Inside they do not know why they have a problem with us and they curse us under their breath all the time. That is a level of persecution that intensifies the closer we get to God. Some may say, I thought the closer I got to God that it would be easier. In one sense it will, but in another sense it will not.

The Greek word for meek, *praus*, means: mild or humble. Therefore, it carries the meaning of humility. Humility is an absolute essential quality if we are to walk with the Lord and inherit the earth. Meekness also manifests as a cloak in the spirit realm and angels see it. They know immediately our level of love for God and our level of maturity. The more that we are clothed with the garment of meekness, the more we can be clothed with the power of the ages to come. For true Kingdom authority is clothed in humility.

James 4:6

But he giveth more grace. Wherefore he saith, God resisteth the proud, but giveth grace unto the humble.

He is giving us something! His ability – His power and strength, not just favor. We may not have the sustaining power or spiritual growth to get through what we are presently facing. But grace given at that time, will get us through it every time, until it becomes a sustaining part of who we are. Just because we are having difficulty does not mean that grace is not applied. God allows the enemy to do what is necessary to access and expose the shortcomings in our lives.

God Resists the Proud

God resists the proud but gives grace to the humble. When we are in a difficulty – in a pinch, when we are going through the midst of tribulation and temptation, most likely, there is internal suffering and external suffering. There may be someone on the outside who is really not our problem, but we respond to them as if they are our problem. We have to watch that because in that moment we are going to have our biggest struggle with pride, and that is when we need God's grace the most. This is why many believers stumble and do not overcome the obstacles that have been left in their path. It is why many have setbacks in their lives again, and again, because the problem is not who the devil is using at the moment, but the problem lies within their unrefined soul. So God opposes the proud, it has a way of expressing itself on our countenance. The scriptures say that God's Word will strengthen us, settle us and bring us to a place of calmness.

It may not be the time when God will go after the root, instead, He may be just pruning. That is what the husbandman does so that we may become more fruitful. God wants a harvest from us and He knows how to get it. He has no problem with us feeding off of the life that is within us. That is an important aspect of becoming like Him. But we must be a doer and not just a hearer. Our purpose and destiny involve doing. It is a whole lot easier when we are doing it out of His life.

We will find out that humility is one of the highest attributes in the Kingdom of heaven. It will take us to a place where literally death will not affect us, if it is not the will of God. Death is the last enemy that we put under our feet. Death will be swallowed up by the life that is in us. And every message that Christ Our Lord gave in the Gospels came from these beatitudes. Peter tells us that we are transformed, we are changed, we are partakers of His divine nature through revelation knowledge.

The remaining five beatitudes are no good to us without humility. That is why Christ Our Lord preceded them with humility. If we had the rest of them without humility, we would lose it all. Christians who are not rooted and grounded on the inside of them with these Kingdom principles, will find in these last days that the cares of this life, the deceitfulness of riches, the lust of other things will choke what they have in them.

In order to progress in our Christian life, there is the need for meekness. Meekness is viewed by the world as a weakness or a lack of strength of character. In modern terms, we could say what the world considers "a push-over" or one who is easily taken advantage of or defeated. However, in God's eyes meekness is a precious character trait. Peter says that *"... a meek and quiet spirit, which is in the sight of God of great price"* (1 Peter 3:4). Meekness is not weakness, but strength under control. It is the strength of character that enables us not to retaliate or defend ourselves.

Meekness is exemplified by the words of Paul in Romans 8:28, *"And we know that all things work together for good to them that love God, to them who are the called according to his purpose."* Those who are meek accept every circumstance that comes their way from the Lord with a rejoicing attitude, realizing that God uses every situation to purify and perfect us. This quality of meekness can be illustrated from Proverbs.

Proverbs 21:1

The king's heart is in the hand of the Lord, as the rivers of water: he turneth it whithersoever he will.

Being meek is the quality of being pliable and easily controlled by the Lord. This is why rebellion is as the sin of witchcraft. The virtue of meekness is so rare, in fact, only two men in the Word of God are called meek: Moses and Christ our Lord. When we are meek, we will yoke ourselves to Christ our Lord and His way of doing things.

Take My Yoke

Matthew 11:29

Take my yoke upon you, and learn of me; for I am meek and lowly in heart: and ye shall find rest unto your souls.

The reward of the meek is that they will inherit the earth. This is repeated in Psalm 37:11. Therefore, to obtain our inheritance, we must cry out to the Lord to work out this beautiful quality in our lives.

My granddad did not have a tractor on his farm, he used a plow. He would take a younger animal and yoke it with an older animal. In doing so, he would teach the younger one how to keep time, and what to do. This is what Christ our Lord wants to do with us, but we have to take the yoke from Him and put it around our own neck. The yoke is an aspect of the Cross; they go hand in hand, because the moment we take God's

Word and start learning of Him, Satan comes immediately to take the Word that is sown. We are thrust into a spiritual war the moment we make an attempt to transform our lives – to become like Him, so we can build a firm foundation.

The enemy often comes while we are in the midst of getting more revelation. He does not wait until we have the whole counsel that we need in a matter, but he comes to steal, kill and destroy that revelation. We will hear based upon our level of spiritual maturity, and we must remember that the Lord is humble and we are not! We are always finding ways to break free from His yoke. He is not going to lock us into His yoke, we have to make a choice to do that ourselves. And when we do, we shall find rest unto our soul. That is our biggest problem and our biggest battle lies within our soul life. The Lord is saying, "I have the key. I have the answer that will bring purity to your soul, but you have to yoke yourself to Me.

Meekness is a Mindset

Galatians 5:23

Meekness, temperance: against such there is no law.

Meekness is not just a cloak; it is a presence and a mindset. And we have temperance to help us constrain the flesh. For they that are in Christ have crucified the flesh of the affections and lusts.

Paul tells us to crucify our flesh because it is our flesh life that is feeding from our soul. And the pressure our soul is putting on our flesh to bend – to bow, is only broken when we humble ourselves before God. We have to train ourselves to look within and not to look outward.

We have to be really wise or the enemy will cause us to miss what the problem really is in our lives. And then we miss an opportunity for the husbandman to extract and the problem is embedded deeper within our soul. It may be a day, a year, or two years before the Holy Spirit addresses it again and we will go around that mountain again and again.

We cannot approach God's Word without meekness. James tells us, "Humble yourself therefore under the mighty hand of God so that He may exalt you in due time." We cannot understand God's Word unless He enlightens us. So if God is resisting us, then we are going to have a problem being enlightened.

James 1:21

Wherefore lay apart all filthiness and superfluity of naughtiness, and receive with meekness the engrafted word, which is able to save your souls.

When he is speaking of an aspect of filthiness, he is talking about both flesh and spirit. The moment people think of flesh they immediately think of sexual sin. There is more to fleshly things than our sexual appetites. Anything that is against God's Word is filthiness. So lay aside, set apart filthiness, superfluidity of naughtiness, and receive with meekness the engrafted word, which is able to save, deliver and set us free.

Our Soul Needs Saved

Because our soul needs saving, the Word becomes engrafted inside of us, it becomes a part of us. It has to be engrafted because it does not always take root when planted within our souls. God will be either pruning, uprooting or planting in our lives. This dear brothers and sisters is why it is a process, and why we are either failing or passing when it comes time to take our tests. Part of our destiny is to inherit some things upon this earth but we cannot do it without meekness.

The Bible says the earth was given to Adam but through sin he gave it to Lucifer. And the Kingdom of God suffered violence and we have to take everything by force. Christ Our Lord gave us the keys of the Kingdom. We have the keys, but when we tell Lucifer he has to go, what do we think he is going to do? He will resist us at every turn. But when we are equipped internally with a firm foundation, the enemy will not have a hope of prevailing against us.

Titus 3:2

To speak evil of no man, to be no brawlers, but gentle, shewing all meekness unto all men.

We cannot enter into this promise, unless we become meek in personality and character. This is what tests and trials are all about, where the Potter is smoothing out all the rough places in our lives. We get saved and think our future is ahead of us; then God immediately starts working on our past. If we do not let Him do so, we end up pulling all that luggage around like dead weight, causing us to never walk as deep and high in the eternal purpose and destiny for our lives. Some of our old baggage has been packed away for a long time and it is moth ridden and smells. But then the Lord comes along with a nice test and pops the lid on it. We smell it and so does everyone else, because it comes out through our actions. Others around us find themselves the recipients of our not very graceful ways. Hint, hint we have to kick in our own humility. This is where iron sharpens iron. We happen to be the ones though who are swinging the iron, yet, we too are getting our iron sharpened while others swing theirs around.

Let Patience have Its Perfect Work

For most, it may not appear at the moment that we will be better off by letting patience have its perfect work, but we will be. When we approach a brother or sister, and we did not have a good day or whatever the reason, or we come to church and something within us just wants to lay into them, but we hold it and do not lash out at them. When we walk away, we have won that battle over the flesh. It is easy to tell people off, but it is a different ball game when we discipline the flesh to submit to the Spirit.

Many Christians will not swing their fists in church, but we do not mind swinging our tongue. We speak our 20 words before somebody else has one word. But James tells us to speak no evil of any man. Well, Pastor it is true, we may say. Remember, if it does not pass the sift test, we cannot do it. Whatsoever things are honest, whatsoever things are true, whatsoever things are lovely. Does it qualify? Does it pass the test? It may be true, but it is not lovely. Someone may be a fool, but who's being satisfied by saying it? Nobody but ourselves. Does it make our flesh feel better? It does do that, but where will that get us? James said, speak evil of no man. To be no brawlers. We are to be gentle with one another. Do not let anybody ring our bell, meaning manipulate your emotions. Do not be wearing it on our shoulders.

Colossians 3:12-13

Put on therefore, as the elect of God, holy and beloved, bowels of mercies, kindness, humbleness of mind, meekness, longsuffering; Forbearing one another, and forgiving one another, if any man have a quarrel against any: even as Christ forgave you, so also do ye.

Put on therefore, as the elect of God, holy and beloved, bowels of mercies, meekness, humility. That means when God makes that available to us through breaking us, then we have to put it on. We have to make ourselves available for the test and trial. We have to be willing to go through it His way, if we are going to put it on. Somebody is going to ruffle our feathers. It is going to be difficult. We have to be willing to let the Potter mold and shape us into His character.

The Potter Breaks Us in the Right Season

We all have flaws and if the Lord waited until we were all perfect to use us, there would not be anyone to use! The Potter reaches into our lives and breaks us in the right season and time. He starts molding us into His character. We have to be willing to stay on the Potter's wheel and quit jumping off. Notice when a little water is put on the clay, it makes it a whole lot easier to shape it. That represents the times of refreshing that comes from the presence of the Lord.

Humbleness is nothing without kindness. We are to put on a humbleness of mind, meekness with longsuffering. If we have the wrong perception of somebody, we are going to respond to them accordingly. To be humble of mind means that we are not looking at the other person's faults. How long are we to suffer? Until we get through it, forbearing with one another. That means to put up with one another, but we have to do so with kindness. We can think that we did a good job because we got through a conversation without cussing someone out, but we know that we were not kind in doing so. The good news, we will get the opportunity again to get better at it so that we may pass our tests.

The life of Christ is taking hold within your soul. Do not condemn yourself, or beat yourself up if you miss it. When you do, you will simply be giving the devil the final blow. Why? Because he will stop your momentum. You will find that you cannot even receive your repentance by faith with condemnation. And because you are too condemned, you want to believe he heard your repentance.

Put on Love

If any man has a quarrel against any, even as Christ forgave you also do ye. So we have no right to be holding any unforgiveness – any offenses against anyone, ever! Paul says, we are to put on Love.

Colossians 3:14

And above all these things put on charity, which is the bond of perfectness.

What is the attitude of Love? That I am going to treat people the way that I would want to be treated, which is the bond of perfectness. This is what holds everything else together and causes us to be perfected into His Love. This is the fertilizer that must go into the soil of our souls, putting first things first. This is the strength that will cause our foundation to be firm.

* * *

Chapter 4: Hunger & Thirst For Righteousness

We pointed out earlier that a lot of the people of God are going to go under in these coming days because they do not have a good foundation. We have to keep first things first. Matthew's chapter five, six and seven record what theologians call the Sermon on the Mount. Within these teachings, chapter five contains the blessings of the Beatitudes. Everything that Christ Our Lord taught here is what He expounded upon throughout His earthly ministry.

As believers, we should constantly be judging ourselves against these Kingdom requirements. And, not just to the Beatitudes, but also what we call the love chapter – I Corinthians 13. These two chapters should be part of our constant mediation as a Christian, for they will bring us back in line to what heaven is saying as to who we are, and what we are to be like on this earth. Keep this in mind as we move on in our studies, after we graduate from earths school our prom is the marriage supper of the lamb. The millennial reign will consist of our Melchizedek priesthood training, where we will minister to our father face to face and go out from him and minister to his creation in his name.

Very Little Hunger

Matthew 5:6
Blessed are they which do hunger and thirst after righteousness: for they shall be filled.

Many in the Church are compromising truth and do not follow after righteousness, or what is right. Hence, there is very little hunger in people's lives for the things of God. One of the strongest drives given to mankind by God is hunger. Survival instinct, in retrospect to hunger, can be very strong and cause people to do strange things in order not to starve. If we do not have morals, it will push us to steal. Righteous hunger is supposed to drive us towards God. It should compel us to do whatever is necessary for our spiritual growth. When there is none or very little hunger for God, it is why someone will compromise their spiritual life.

As Christians, we should be practicing living right – living in righteousness. In turn, the Holy Spirit will create a hunger in us to do what is right by making it a conscious or unconscious thing in our lives. There is a Kingdom law, which whatever we strongly desire, we will attract it to ourselves. This is a law in the Spirit. It is why we see people attract the very things they do not want into their lives, because inside their soul it is what they strongly desire, with most not realizing it. Because we are not going to get what we say, we are going to get what we believe. This is why the Father allows tests and trials in our lives. Because many do not know what they believe until they are faced with it. Do not get me wrong, speaking and declaring is part of schooling ourselves into faith, but that is just one side of the same coin.

Faith is an act. It is not just declaring we have something. Faith requires that we must get up and do what we are declaring because the two together – faith and our actions, will begin to govern what we believe. With that said, we can make a declaration with our mouths but in the spirit realm demons can see what we actually believe. And what we believe is what we attract. It is like this; the spirit realm is pictorial and demons are looking at us from that realm. When they see lust floating past them, it then can attach itself to us, if we have issues with lust. They know what we believe because we are attracting it. They do not have to read our mind; it is very plain for them to see in the spirit realm.

The Law of Attraction

The law of attraction impacts very much what we are hungering for, it is a powerful law. Kids today think that whatever they touch in the natural realm will not affect them in the spirit realm. Unless we get them to believe God's Word, they are going to keep attracting the wrong thing, because they have demonic spirits working against them, and not just their flesh. The immoral stuff that they get their hands on, most of it is pictorial in nature and this is why the enemy likes it. Movies and video games are full of death and violence. Words paint pictures in our minds. We do not see in words; we see in pictures. If I say dog, you do not see the words dog. Instead, if you have a dog, you see your dog in your mind. If you do not have a dog, the mind is so powerful that it will search the archives of your mind and find one! If I say black dog, the picture starts getting sharper and it changes. The archives of your mind will start searching for a black dog. Our minds are like a computer hard drive, where it stores pieces of information from things that we have seen over the years, and can bring forth a black dog in our mind.

In the same way, for every analogy in the natural realm there is a spiritual one. Because that is where it comes from. Remember the story of Snow White. Mirror, mirror on the wall who is the fairest of them all. Snow White believed she was the fairest of them all. So she expected to see her picture to come up on the mirror. But one day someone else's picture comes on the mirror instead. Believe it or not it is the same way with people today. If a literal mirror was a reflection of the spirit realm of what is actually looking back at them, it would shock the hell out of them. In other words what they have given their life to is what they are attracting. This is why what we think upon is so powerful because it shapes what we desire, which impacts our hunger, which in turns transforms us into what we become.

This truth is our reality, whether we can see in that realm or not, but most do not understand this spiritual law. We preach it, but people do not believe it. Older people it is your responsibility, as ones who are to know the way, to teach or impact our young generation – this Joel generation; to help them see the reality of the truth. It is not your responsibility to make people see. That is the Holy Spirit's responsibility to get people to see. You just have to put it out there, as He sets up the right circumstances and conditions when they are susceptible and ready to hear. The Lord knows how to bring your voice right back to their head and they will hear it in your voice. A lot of times they have to humble themselves to hear it, then their eyes start to open. Did not God say He gives grace to the humble? Part of that grace is enabling them to see.

A Spiritual Connection

Hence, this spiritual law has far reaching consequences. Because the connection that we make in what we focus on, it is a spiritual connection and that is what most do not understand. That is where the power of meditation affects us for good or evil. Did you know that watching TV is a mild form of mediation? Because when we do, our focus is on what we are looking at. Then our mind goes to that place, as we try to figure it out. That is what meditation is, and this is why even what we watch is so important. Most TV programs today are there to release a message or to do what it says, program you. This is why it is called programming.

In a new TV trailer, I saw this statement that orange is the new black and they call it the Modern Family. It is about two gay men living together and a young girl who is a lesbian. In other words, they are releasing the message that this is the new family now. This is their definition of family and putting

46

it in the form of a comedy. It is from these types of things where people form what they call their favorite TV show. Not realizing that they are being programmed and their desires or what they hunger for are slowly being changed, with them becoming an enemy of the cross

When I was a kid the big thing that older people watched were the soap operas. I would come home from school and hear my mom talk about it like it was something that happened in real life. A show about adultery, fornication, backbiting, sedition and murder. This was the message coming through the TV screen, yet everyone knew it as just a program. But Christ our Lord taught from the parable of the sower that when the seed goes into the ground, the ground does not determine the validity of the seed. It accepts whatever is put into it. Our heart is no different. When we sow the filth and lusts of this world into our lives by watching such programs, we are laying a foundation within our souls that will grow and fight against the very things that we should be believing.

What We Believe Determines What We Hunger and Thirst After

It is like advertisers. Are they going to waste billions of dollars on advertising that does not work? Or, like our computers that drop cookies leaving a trail of our preferences that are stored on the websites that we have visited. Ever wonder why, when we have not been to one of those websites in a while, we see advertisements trying to get us to go back to those websites. And, amazing, they chose the word cookie meaning who can resist sweets? Well, all truths are parallel; it reflects the very things that are happening in that realm around us. Demon's track what goes on in our lives. Demons come after us through the cares of this world, the deceitfulness of riches and by the lusts of other things that they drop inside of us, just like cookies on a computer. What we watch, see, hear, read, replays on the screen of our souls, ultimately impacting what we believe that will determine what we hunger and thirst after.

Dearly beloved brothers and sisters, we must understand what is going on around us. We are making spirit connections all the time. We connect with the power behind the object of our focus. That is why pornography is so deadly and dangerous. I saw on Computer News where there was a 22- or 23-year-old martial arts teacher who was sending nude pictures to an 11-year-old. She kept telling him, I like you; I want to be with you. Where do you think she got that spirit in her? I guarantee you it was from watching pornography. This thing that used to be mainly a strong hold of men is now finding its way into the life of women. The person who wrote the article quickly pointed out the fact that he did not think the article got 20 million hits because of what she did. It got 20 million hits because of the response of the young man. It is parents' responsibility to be determining what their kids believe, not some video game, movie or even teacher at school.

Mark 11:24

Therefore I say unto you, What things soever ye desire, when ye pray, believe that ye receive them, and ye shall have them.

Among the many things that Christ our Lord taught here, He

emphasizes if we are to be filled with righteousness, we have to hunger for it. Desire is fueled by hunger. It is determined by what we believe and it does not matter what it is, we will have it. The spirit world will see to it, for it is a spiritual law. That is why so many Christians are filled with so many things of this world that are destroying their lives.

Imputed and Imparted Righteousness

It is those who hunger and thirst after righteousness that will be filled. There are two kinds of righteousness: imputed and imparted. When we accept Christ as our Savior, we are counted righteous in His sight (Romans 3:22). In other words, His righteousness is imputed to us. However, there is a further degree of righteousness that the Lord wants to bring us into – imparted righteousness, which means that His righteousness is actually worked into our lives so that we are righteous as He is (1 John 3:7). We will receive the gift of His righteousness (Psalm 24:5). As Christians, we will be filled with whatever we long for and desire, whether it is good or bad. But if we hunger and thirst after righteousness, and allow the Lord to transform us into His image so that we are righteous and straight as He is, then at the end of our lives, we will receive the crown of righteousness. Therefore imparted righteousness comes through righteousness acts which are a result of being a doer of the word.

* * *

Chapter 5: Blessed Are The Merciful

Matthew 5:7

Blessed are the merciful: for they shall obtain mercy.

The Sermon on the Mount is very profound in the sense that every letter of the law, every spiritual thought, teaching, principle or doctrine that the disciples ever spoke about, I believe they got it from these teachings from Christ our Lord. For He laid the foundation or doctrinal teaching for today, and the disciples simply built upon it.

Everything We Need is within the Seed

So when talking about building a foundation or sowing the seed and reaping a harvest, everything that we need is found within the seed. We are saying the same thing just using a little different language. All that we have to do is plant the seed, knowing that the root and the substance in which it needs to grow is in the seed. However, the seed must die in order to live and bring forth fruit. We may be a student of the Word and read it year after year, but we need to ask this question: if the Word of God is not coming alive on the inside of me, am I dying to self so that it may live within my soul? Why ask? Because every time the Word of God brings forth revelation it challenges our flesh. If we are not being challenged by the Word when we read it, we have not accessed the revelatory realm of the Word. We have the rhema and the logos Word of God. Logos – the written Word, is not any good to us until it becomes a rhema word where the Holy Spirit quickens our spirit with revelation, making it applicable to our current situation.

If we feel condemned once the Word reveals something to us, that is not the Word condemning us, instead that is our flesh. The Word convicts, it does not condemn. Why is this so important? So we do not draw back from truth. Our flesh will condemn so that we will draw back from truth. To come out from the condemnation and stop our flesh from choking the Word that is on the inside of us, we must learn to humble ourselves. We have to understand what is going on and learn to discipline our flesh. If not, we will stay a baby Christian and not grow and mature into His likeness. Our flesh has a voice and we have to learn how to talk to it. Understanding

51

the principles of the Word and how God's Word works, will trigger the life-giving force that is in the Word.

Enter into Him Who is the Door

It will allow the Word to stay on the inside of us and to keep tearing down things in our character and lives that are detrimental to the Kingdom. We do this by surrendering our will for His will, for that is our part to do. In our new birth, we welcomed Him in through the house of our heart. Now, we must learn to enter into Him Who is the Door. There is a whole lot of space we need to explore when it comes to God. So as a believer we need to remove the "do not disturb sign" in our heart. God cannot do that for He will not go against our will. One of the ways we do that is to become a student of the Word. At the same time, we can only get by so far with our baby prayers, "Lord help me, I really need You to help me. I really need You to do this for me." God, by His grace, will do that when we are a legitimate baby, but He is not an enabler! When all of our faculties are working and we are well able to read the Word and come to the house of God; He will not keep doing that when we are supposed to be growing. The Word of God is so fruitful and alive, it will literally become food to our soul, causing our spirit man to grow.

In order for us not to become hard, critical and self-righteous, the mercy of God must be worked out in our souls. We must realize that it is only because of God's mercy that we are saved and must look upon others through the eyes of mercy. When we are merciful to others, God will be merciful to us.

Exodus 34:6

And the Lord passed by before him, and proclaimed, The Lord, The Lord God, merciful and gracious, longsuffering, and abundant in goodness and truth,

Psalm 18:25

With the merciful thou wilt shew thyself merciful; with an upright man thou wilt shew thyself upright;

Mercy is a translation of the Hebrew word *"chesed."* It is a very difficult word to translate into

English because it has several meanings and connotations. It describes an outflowing of love, compassion, loving kindness and sympathy for one in need. Mercy is always expressed through actions, and it is always associated with good works. It not only causes us to feel compassion for a person, but it causes us to help the person in need.

James 3:17

But the wisdom that is from above is first pure, then peaceable, gentle, and easy to be intreated, full of mercy and good fruits, without partiality, and without hypocrisy.

Freely We are to Give

The Greek word for mercy is *"éleos."* It means to be compassionate by word or deed. It also means divine grace. One of the words for mercy is grace or grace extended. The Bible tells us freely we have received, freely we are to give. The world will get much more grace directly from us than from God because it flows through us, from God to them.

Why does God bring healing into the Body of Christ? So that we can go heal the world – the lost, sick and downtrodden, with the same healing that we have received. The Bible says that healing is the children's bread. In the same way we get bread to eat with our meals, it is meant to be automatic. Healing is ours; it is our bread. So, we are not the sick trying to be healed, instead we should be the healed who are maintaining our health. Because in this natural world the enemy has learned how to cause diseases to impact our bodies, and then we can do stupid things that impact our bodies well-being. Nevertheless, healing is ours – it is our daily bread that is to be eaten.

How many of us, given the opportunity, have ever laid our hands on someone and said, "Can I pray for you?" If we never avail ourselves to others, why does God need to avail Himself to us? If we never allow the healing power of God to flow through us, then what good are we to God? Mark 16 says that we are to lay hands on the sick and they shall recover. Some may say, "But how do I know if God will do it?" Our job is to pray and believe for their healing and let God do His part. He is the healer. It is impossible to please Him without faith and faith without works is dead faith. So all we have to do is avail our hands when given the opportunity and lay them on the sick to be healed. Somebody has to have some faith to do it, so it might as well be you! So, if you see someone in need, ask if you can pray for them. Then just pray and do not be concerned about what if, amen!

Another reason God has healing in the Church is to give people an opportunity to believe in Him. Healing is the dinner bell. Christ Our Lord turned to the people and said, if you do not believe who I say that I am, then believe Me for the works' sake. I believe the reason the world is not being won over is there is no proof of God in His house. The Lord told us to go into the highway and hedges to compel them to come, that His house would be filled. What are we going to compel the lost with so they will come to His House? Is it our looks? No, because if it were many would not be able to get any to come. Is it our money? No, because some of us are broke all the time.

So, what are we going to compel them with? The Word of God, by extending grace. For blessed are the merciful. Blessed are those who receive grace for they shall release grace. Mercy means to have compassion. It will be very hard to reach out to the world when we are overly consumed with our own problems. We do not have to be that way, for He told us to cast all of our cares upon Him.

Created for God's Love to Flow

We were created for God's love to flow through us. But we have to position ourselves and become doers, as we are commanded to do so. We need to allow God's love to come out of us when we see someone that needs God's Love. If we connect with God on the inside, a power will rise up on the inside of us and we can release that to whoever heaven wants to have it. As an ambassador to heaven, that is one of our kingly roles as one's who sit with Him in heavenly places, to represent heaven on earth.

When the devil has his feet on our neck and we are hurting, most become self-centered. Whether it is the devil directly or he is doing it through someone else. The greatest lesson we can learn from our Lord is when we are hurting the most, that is the greatest opportunity to allow compassion or mercy to flow out of us. He will certainly bring healing to our own lives speedily. It is also the best time to crush the devil's head. For when we hurt the most, if we allow that pain to become the anointing of release for someone else, then we can slap the devil in the head. Satan does not want us to release the power of compassion to bring healing. He will think twice before making a move towards us like that again

Mercy describes the act, while compassion describes the feelings that accompany the act. I remember quite a few years ago, I was ministering to a mother with a child who was sick. When I saw the child, I thought of my own child and all of a sudden, these tears welled up on the inside of me and I began to weep. I had recognized the first time it happened that it was the Lord. Within compassion is also pity, but not human pity that only feels sorry for someone, but cannot move the problem. When compassion releases divine pity, there is healing power behind it. When I was with that mother, I took the baby out of her hands and the baby was healed. God wants to do that through us all the time but the enemy wants to keep us disconnected. Christ Our Lord said, we are to be light, a beacon that sits on a hill bringing hope to a dying world.

Our Hurting World

Every time we leave our house, we should be scanning on the inside asking, "Father, how do You want to use me today?" We need to leave our own hurting world behind and look at the hurting world around us. We are the ones who are free with the love of God flowing through us. We are the closest thing to heaven that the lost or broken are going to ever see. If we do not avail ourselves, then why should the Father give Himself to us? I was in a meeting one time with a man of God. The power of God started moving on this young man who was on the worship team. When the power of God fell upon him, he began to yell and scream, run, shout and dance. The man of God looked at him and said, "Son, you just dissipated the power." The young man did not know what he was talking about and the man explained to him how that power came on him to bring healing to someone in the congregation.

Now, there are times that the Holy Spirit simply falls on someone and releases healing power. In this case though, the Holy Spirit chose to flow through someone leading worship and that person missed it. The laying on of hands is not the only way the scriptures teach healing, so we need to be sensitive to the Holy Spirit. God will do more through us in the marketplace than in the Church. If we go out with this purpose in mind, "Lord, who do you want to touch, who do you want to speak to, who do you want to prophesy to, who do you want to heal today?" That mindset causes a demand to be made on heaven and heaven will start downloading His mercy and love through us.

During Christ our Lord time of prayer, The Bible says it is a great while before day. He talked to the Father and was shown by the Holy Spirit all that the Father desired for Him to do for that day. Christ Our Lord would see Himself do those things in vision, then go act them out. That is why He said, "I only do that which I see My Father do, and say what I hear Him say." If

57

we do what Christ Our Lord did, then we can have the same results He had and even greater, because He has gone to the Father. Did He not say go out into the highways and byways and compel them to come? I heard a true story from a friend of mine who went before the Lord for the healing of a young lady. He asked the Lord why He would not heal this woman's child, for she was not sinning or living an unholy life. But Christ our Lord looked at him and asked, "What is she doing for My Kingdom? She is My child, but she is no profit to Me or My Kingdom."

My friend was then made to remember the parable of where Christ our Lord was walking through that garden looking for fruit and could not find any. The Father told the husbandman – or keeper of the garden, who is Christ Our Lord to cut it down, saying "Why let it take up space?" In other words, He is saying, it is a waste of space, dig it up and throw it away for it is useless. But the husbandman begs Him to give it one more year to let him dig around it and fertilize it. If it does not produce fruit, then He will cut it down.

God Expects Good Fruit from Our Lives

Brothers and sisters, Christ our Lord is talking about you and I! God expects good fruit to come forth from our lives. He expects a harvest. We cannot be takers – users and abusers of His goodness and mercy, and not do anything with it! I submit to you; He will be removing many in these last days. We are at the door of the great falling away. Most do not have what it takes within them to withstand the darkness that is coming, instead they will succumb to it. Our Father wants to release His mercy and love through us in these last days to be a light to the lukewarm Church before it is too late, and to bring in the harvest.

The great falling away will soon begin and much sacrifice by us will cause many to cry out to Him for help. The prophet Isaiah forewarned that gross darkness will cover the earth and the people. When gross darkness comes, people will start doing things that they would not normally have done in the day time. They will do things that they used to do only during the night hours. Look at the darkness presently moving across our nation. People are coming out boldly now and not just the gays with their LGBTQ+ agenda, but the killing of babies that are in the womb and even changing the consent of age to do so. Because the darkness is pressing in and pushing them out into the open – into daylight. That same darkness is going to start pressing against the people of God and we better have enough light to repel it or we will end up in compromise. Hence; the great falling away.

Remember the young lady, who was His child yet he told His servant that she was of no use to Him. My friend told her what Christ our Lord had spoken to him. Do you know what she did? She started going to the homes of old people and passed out tracks and read scriptures to them. She started doing something in the Kingdom of God. She started availing herself and became useful to the King. The Lord later told him to tell her exactly how many years He would add to her life. The scripture says, "Seek ye first the Kingdom of God and His righteousness and everything else you need will be added to you." Seeking the Kingdom is what God wants us to be doing first and foremost. When we do, everything that we need to carry out that day will be added to us. God will automatically take care of our needs.

Being a Doer to Become Like Him

In being merciful or showing mercy I have attempted to convey the emphasis is being a doer. It was the doer's house that stood. The second part of that equation is becoming like Him in our character. That is the most difficult part because it requires death. We can be religious and keep doing our church activities and duties, yet not die to the flesh and be in a position to obtain mercy. God has already determined what we need to embrace in order to enable us to become like Him.

Blessed are the compassionate – the merciful, for they shall receive compassion. Remember mercy describes the act and compassion describes the feeling that accompanies the act. That is why we have to be neutral when it comes to people. That is why God is endeavoring to always change what we believe concerning things because it affects our actions and our feelings. When God wants compassion to flow through us – for our heart to break for someone, and we believe something negative concerning that person, He cannot do what He wants to do in their life or in ours. Remember, the person that irks us the most could be the very one who God wants to bring breakthrough to through us. This is why the enemy makes things so difficult. In the same way, the relationship that is the most important to us will be the one most difficult to hold on to. What am I saying? That we need one another.

God determined that we should impact each other's lives. There are people that come into our lives for seasons. There are people that come into our lives for a minute or so, but then there are people that will be in our lives throughout eternity. So we must learn to recognize when a relationship is the hardest – the most difficult, what the enemy is trying to do and why. Many times, what we have on the inside of us is the very thing that person will need to turn or change. And if we walk away from that relationship because of hurt feelings or ill will, we will not overcome, instead we will have walked away with the very life God gave us to impart to them. Then God will have to raise up someone else to get the job done and that simply prolongs their deliverance and ours.

I will keep repeating things in this book because it is my style of teaching, plus repetitiveness is a must for humans. So mercy describes the act and compassion is the power and feeling that accompanies the act. The Lord will dump a portion of what He feels concerning something on the inside of us and that feeling will keep us on course until compassion has run its course. Remember the scriptures said Christ Our Lord was moved with compassion and He healed them all. His feelings, in that moment, were impacted to the degree, level and time until deliverance came to every single person, then it was shut off. Learning how to flow and how to yield to the Holy Spirit is very important in this hour that we live. Because there is a world out there that desperately needs Christ Our Lord with many not knowing they need Him. So showing mercy is not a legalistic or judicial act, it is something that God said we must do. It is generated as a feeling, a yearning to ease the suffering and the difficulty that a person has gotten themselves into. This is why we must get beyond our own hurts and needs, and go minister to someone who is hurting.

Take on Someone Else's Pain

It is not that our hurts and needs are not important to God for He cares about every detail of our lives, but when we walk in mercy towards others, despite our own hurt and sufferings, then God can move us past where we are and take us deeper into His eternal purposes. So that means we have to get up by faith and put our hurts aside and take on someone else's pain. The time that we hurt the most, will be one of the most powerful times of our lives to alleviate someone else's suffering. We see that principle in the scripture. If we really want to hurt the enemy, reach out and try to impact somebody else's life while our own lives are hurting the most. Mercy, which is an attribute of the Holy Spirit's power, will flow through us and bring deliverance to somebody in need. And while it is flowing through us, it will heal us.

Remember, went Christ our Lord into the wilderness alone because He was hurting. His best friend was dead because of some sexual, lustful stupid act. So how did He get comfort? By going around and stomping on the devil by bringing mercy and healing to all those around Him who were hurting. I guarantee you He was refreshed afterwards! That is how it works.

So that inner yearning – or feeling, triggers compassion, which releases the power or the ability of God to help someone else. It is more than just a feeling. It is more than just emotion. It is a power that flows through our inner man. Locked within that feeling that is moving around on the inside of us, is a power waiting to be released. That power could be healing; it could be the anointing to cast out a devil. It could be an anointing to break something off of someone's mind or thought life, so we must be very, very sensitive to the Holy Spirit and how he wants to flow through us.

Matthew 9:36

But when he saw the multitudes, he was moved with compassion on them, because they fainted, and were scattered abroad, as sheep having no shepherd.

If we want to connect with the power of God very quickly, be moved by someone else's plight. That means getting our eyes off ourselves and be ready to advance the Kingdom. As we move throughout life or wherever we find ourselves, learn to be moved by someone else's plight. When we do, we will draw the power of God like a magnet to steel because God loves people. He wants to bring relief to people, especially those outside of the Church. Christ our Lord said to them again and again, if you do not believe me for what I say, believe me for the work's sake.

Heaven's Power and Ability

Matthew 14:14

And Jesus went forth and saw a great multitude and was moved with compassion.

He knew He could not help them without the power of the Holy Spirit. He was no longer God. But He made a demand on heaven's power and ability. That means there was something intuitive that happened and He initiated it. He went forth and He saw, then was moved but He knew that was not enough and it pulled the power of God upon Him where He could do something about it. The enemy's objective is to get us lost in our own little hurts and our own little worlds so that we care less about what is going on around us. To the degree that he can do that; he will shut down the power of God to the world because we are the light of the world. It was the Lord who told us to go into the highways and hedges and compel people to come into His house.

Christ our Lord had a set time period to do what He was sent to do. He made good use of His time on the earth by constantly thinking about touching people's lives with heaven's redemptive and restorative power, and by fulfilling the will of His Father. We do not realize how important we are to the Kingdom. The reason being many have not found purpose, and where there is no purpose, there is no vision. And without vision people perish. If we become insensitive to the hurting world around us, we will fail to attract the power of God to deliver or bring healing to someone.

Mark 1:41

And Jesus, moved with compassion, put forth His hand, and touched him, and saith unto him, I will; be thou clean.

Notice He did not put forth His hand until He was moved with compassion. And when He did, He touched him and said unto him, be clean. Christ our Lord was working hand in hand with the Holy Spirit, while He was moving hand in hand with His emotions, and He knew He was helpless without the Holy Spirit.

Release the Flow of God's Ability

1 John 3:17

But whoso hath this world's good, and seeth his brother have need, and shutteth up his bowels of compassion from him, how dwelleth the love of God in him?

Now the Lord brings it to another level. He is not talking about the world; He is talking about those in the house of God. About those who see that their brother has a need yet shut off their bowels of compassion from him. We may want to ask, how does the love of God dwell in our lives? The love of God pulsates thoughts out of our bellies and pushes it through our bowels – or bellies, by compassion. Many see the need but either look the other way or say I will loan it to you. What if they cannot pay it back? One of the major strongholds in our lives is pride and part of pride is self-interest that asks, "What will I get in exchange, if I give this to you?" But every time the love of God flows through us, it will purify us.

The feeling and emotions of compassion are required to release the flow of God's ability in the gifts of the Spirit. We see Christ Our Lord yielding to it all the time. I want to keep emphasizing it was God's love flowing through Him that caused Him to be drawn to compassion. Christ Our Lord loved people. It did not matter what they did, what they said or where they came from. When it was necessary, He rebuked them but He still loved them.

This is one of the reasons that we do not see mass healings and deliverances around us, because we lack God's love for people. Every time we connect a scripture of compassion with

Christ our Lord , everyone that was in His presence was healed, delivered and set free. When He could not access all of them that way, He had to fall back on the gifts of healing or the healing anointing, by touching one or two and then walking away leaving the rest unhealed. But Christ Our Lord made sure that He availed Himself to mercy and compassion.

Showing mercy or compassion also has the meaning of: being without judgment. Improperly judging people will shut it down every time. If God tells us to give $500 to someone and we look at them based on what they have, we will not give it. Mercy helps us to let go of judgment so it can flow. I remember a story that a preacher was telling about a woman who was a multi-millionaire but when it came to God she was not very giving. She thought everyone was out to use and abuse her. You know how God broke that spirit off of her? Someone gave her a gift of $500 and she broke down and cried and cried, because this person knew she did not need it. But God told her to give it to her and it broke that spirit off of her. God knows what is needed and knows how to set people free.

Do Not Judge

Christ our Lord clearly tells us not to judge one another. What does that mean? When we try to look inwardly into a person's heart and determine why they do what they do. Outwardly, we are to judge the fruit that comes forth in a person's life because if we are to know them that labor among us, we must. But we cannot determine why someone does what they do without the Holy Spirit revealing the motives of their heart, therefore; we are not to judge the heart of man.

Matthew 7:1-2

Judge not, that ye be not judged. For with what judgment ye judge, ye shall be judged: and with what measure ye mete, it shall be measured to you again.

We need to know that the spiritual law of sowing and reaping is always working in our lives and it will come back and bite us if we sow sparingly, or not at all. The way we lay into somebody, then someone else will come along and lay into us, as we have done unto others. God will make sure that we recognize it when it happens. Hence, we reap what we sow. Christ our Lord meant exactly what He said. Do not judge.

Romans 14:10

But why dost thou judge thy brother? or why dost thou set at nought thy brother? for we shall all stand before the judgment seat of Christ.

Mercy cannot flow through us unless we set aside judgment.

James 4:11

Speak not evil one of another, brethren. He that speaketh evil of his brother, and judgeth his brother, speaketh evil of the law, and judgeth the law: but if thou judge the law, thou art not a doer of the law, but a judge.

James tells us not to speak evil of one another. When we speak evil of someone, judging them will follow suit. He is speaking about the law of love because love covers a multitude of sin. We like to think that we know human behavior, except when it comes to our own. Often, we will start by saying what we heard or what we saw or what we think. Let me share a secret though, we can look at a sin in one person and see the same sin in another person, but the reason – or motive, for why they sin can be different. Because we are all different and what makes one person tick is not necessarily what makes someone else tick. So if we are judging the law, we are judging the Law Giver who is God. There is one Law Giver Who is able to save and to destroy. And what is He saying? Do not judge anyone because we cannot save anyone, because we did not die for them!

We cannot know why a person does what they do, unless the Holy Spirit shows us. And according to the Holy Spirit, nine times out of ten, we would do worse. We must remember the saying, "You will never make your light brighter by trying to put out someone else's." We do not want to lend our judgment to darkness and become part of the accuser. This is why many fall and do not recover, because we do not pray for them. We do not have mercy. Paul says in Galatians 6:1, "Brethren, if a man be overtaken in a fault, ye which are spiritual, restore such a one in the spirit of meekness." When we do, we will obtain mercy and not be tempted. We must take on the attitude that the same thing could happen to us. Unless we walk in someone else's shoes, we have no right to talk.

Now I am going to share something personal; I went through a divorce. And when Benny Hinn started having a hard time with his family and his wife left him, what I heard people say about him broke my heart. Not knowing what was happening in his case did not matter to me because I too had walked a similar way. And because of what it does to you, my heart broke for him. Every time I heard criticism of him, I would say under my breath, "Lord, help him." I was overjoyed when they got back together and remarried. If we are not careful, we will become a part of the accuser and then wonder why the love of God that is shed abroad in our hearts is not releasing the healing power of God into our lives. And not just within our own physical bodies and churches, but equally we are not releasing God's compassion throughout the community where it should be flowing.

Condemning the Guiltless

Matthew 12:7

If you had known what this meaneth, I will have mercy and not sacrifice" you would have not condemned the guiltless.

Christ our Lord said that because we do not have mercy, we condemn the guiltless. It is why it is good for us to have mercy, for we do not want to be condemning anyone.

Luke 6:37

Judge not and ye shall not be judged. Condemn not and ye shall not be condemned. Forgive and you shall be forgiven. This is what I call getting favor from God.

1 Samuel 21:2-6

And David said unto Ahimelech the priest, The king hath commanded me a business, and hath said unto me, Let no man know any thing of the business whereabout I send thee, and what I have commanded thee: and I have appointed my servants to such and such a place. Now therefore what is under thine hand? give me five loaves of bread in mine hand, or what there is present. And the priest answered David, and said, There is no common bread under mine hand, but there is hallowed bread; if the young men have kept themselves at least from women. And David answered the priest, and said unto him, Of a truth women have been kept from us about these three days, since I came out, and the vessels of the young men are holy, and the bread is in a manner common, yea, though it were sanctified this day in the vessel. So the priest gave him hallowed bread: for there was no bread there but the shewbread, that was taken from before the Lord, to put hot bread in the day when it was taken away.

These scriptures show that God does not look at things the way we do. The showbread that was taken from before the Lord to put hot bread in the day when it was taken away. There was a time that Saul did it, and now David is doing the same thing. What was the difference? Why did God see it differently although the situations seem to be exactly the same? Remember Rahab at the battle of Jericho, she was a prostitute and how she had lied and hid the spies, that God rewarded her greatly. Now I know all religious spirits have a problem with that fact, but God not only saved her family, she is in the genealogy of Christ Our Lord over a lie! I am simply pointing out that we must see things the way God sees them. Here is another one: God forgave David for his adultery but killed the man who tried to steady the Ark of the Covenant. We would have done the reverse.

Constantly Availing Ourselves to Mercy

So keep in mind, blessed are the merciful for they shall obtain mercy. This is why the Sermon on the Mount is so important. Christ our Lord was laying down the ground rules of how the Kingdom of God operates so that we can build a firm foundation in our lives. This is how we should govern our lives by constantly availing ourselves to mercy. It is something that is very easy to access during intercession, if you are an intercessor who yields to the spirit of travail. Why? Because the Holy Spirit dumps His emotions into ours during intercession, causing strong tears of compassion to flow.

According to 1 Chronicles 21, David knew that God looked at things very differently than man did. When given a choice as to whether he would be handed over to man or to God for judgment, he quickly chose God. In verse 13, David said unto God, "I am in a great straight." It had to do with David taking a census of Israel. When I read that story the first time, I had wondered what was the big deal, why was God so mad at him? He was so angry because David made the mistake of putting his trust in the strength of his army, instead of in the might of the Lord

So, Gad, the prophet comes along with a word of rebuke for David, and David says, "Let me fall now into the hand of the Lord; for very great are His mercies: but let me not fall into the hand of man." This is another reason why God allows us to go through tests and trials – to teach us mercy, or how to be merciful.

Colossians 3:12-13

Put on therefore, **(our responsibility)** as the elect of God, holy and beloved, bowels of mercies, kindness, humbleness of mind, meekness, longsuffering; forbearing one another **(putting up with one another),** and forgiving one another, if any man have a quarrel against any: **(if we have a problem with anyone, we do not have the right to hold a grudge)** even as Christ forgave you, so also do ye."

Our forgiving should not be based upon anyone asking us. We should forgive anyway because we were forgiven, right?

Colossians 3:14

And above all these things put on charity **(love),** which is the bond of perfectness.

Love is the bond, the glue, the mortar that will perfect us into His likeness. Now we see why there is very little maturity in the Church. The very things we should be doing to mature, are not happening in most Christians lives. I do not care how spiritual someone may feel they are, or how much someone may prophecy, we all are going to mess up and will need mercy. And remember, we reap what we have sown. God is not going to get us out of our time of reaping when we sowed to the flesh and did not walk after the Spirit. Especially, if we did not do anything to rectify it, because at the root of it all is pride.

The moral of the story: mercy is a tool that we need, not only to hold ourselves together but to hold other lives together. Mercy is a tangible, heavenly material that flows through us to bring relief to people that are hurting. If we want to be used that way, we have to be merciful to others. We cannot be a person who is critical or judgmental. If we have a problem with something, we need to control our tongue. If we do not, then the very time that we need God's mercy and cry out for it; He will mock us.

* * *

Chapter 6: Blessed Are The Pure In Heart

We are looking at how to be successful from heaven's perspective and that is by building a firm foundation in our lives. If we are impacting the rest of the Body in the area in which we have been placed, then we are being successful. We have the Holy Spirit who is moving on the inside of us constantly ready to give the aid that we need to be successful. Let us pray that God will purify us of all criticism, anger, jealousy and hatred, so that we may be rooted and grounded in the love of God.

The human heart has four valves: the tricuspid, pulmonary, mitral and aortic. These four valves can represent the four groups of people who inspect us: the world, Satan, the Church and Christ. The Lord Himself, as the Passover Lamb, was inspected by four people: Annas, Caiaphas, Pilate and Herod. Upon His inspection, Christ our Lord was found to be clean and pure. Let us pray that we will be found pure when we are inspected, as well. Jeremiah, one who really understood the heart of man, said in Jeremiah 17:9, *"The heart is deceitful above all things, and desperately wicked: who can know it?"* For it is out of the abundance of our heart that every sin proceeds. The only remedy for a heart that is bent on wickedness is to pray continually to the Lord as King David did in Psalm 51:10, *"Create in me a clean heart, O God and renew a right spirit within me."* David wrote this after his sin with Bathsheba. Let us cry out for purity of heart before we fall into sin – for our foundation to be firm, so that we will be preserved from falling.

Three Levels of Growth

To build a firm foundation, will take us through three levels of growth. The first level is revelation; where we need to know what He is saying so we can act upon it. The Logos must become rhema to our spirit, and what He is speaking to our heart must be perceived in our understanding. The second level is visitation; where God manifests Himself to us. It can be a dream that shows us what God is saying. It may be a vision; where He shows us what He is doing and what He wants us to do. So, it has to go from revelation to visitation in some form or another. The third level is habitation. In habitation the logos or rhema Word of God comes and abides inside of us. Something happens to our heart, not just in the area of hearing but something is deposited inside of us.

Revelation forms around our heart and it starts building a wall of truth within us bringing transformation to our soul, therefore; change to our lives and transforming us as a person who has the image of Christ being built inside of us. Christ our Lord kept a bag that fed the poor and the poor knew it. Many came to Him just so they could eat. When they came, He had a chance to put His word inside of them. He started to build a spiritual wall of truth within them, bringing transformation which in turn brought a visitation. Christ makes up many levels of truth. As we begin feeding upon truth, then Christ is being built up within us in the areas of: love, mercy, giving, forgiveness, grace and in the Fruit of the Spirit. In all these areas, and more, the Holy Spirit is endeavoring to position us to continue that building process.

The moment we come into revelation it begins to become a frame for us, but remember the next level has to be visitation. The Lord will begin to materialize not just as a seed, but as a root; then as a plant and finally as fruit. And with each level truth adds to that growth process. Often, we do not stop and think about who is this Life-giving force Who is making this all possible when we are being transformed into His image. The Holy Spirit, who is being shed abroad in our heart by love, is there to make sure we go on from revelation to visitation by being a doer, or it will not bring about change. In other words, if we do not love enough, we are not going to move from revelation to visitation. Everything can be traced back to this one thing, love. We do what we are doing not because it benefits us, but because we love Him. It must be all about the Kingdom and the King and when it is, we can only benefit from it! The two most important principles in your life will be love and obedience. Christ Our Lord said if you love me do what I say, brothers and sisters talk is cheap when it is not backed up by love, and love can't grow or be shed abroad in our heart without obeying.

Wanting to Please Him

When I started my Christian walk, like most of us, everything that I did was from the mindset of what can I get out of it. As I grew to know the love of God, like the Shunamite woman, it grew to wanting to please Him because I loved Him, not for what He does for me. Even when the Lord asks me to do difficult things, it is easy for me to say yes to Him. I have a conversation with the Lord like this, "Lord, why do You ask me that? You know I cannot say no to You." I am glad that I made my mind up early on that if I was going to walk with Him, it is going to be 100 percent, wide-open full throttle. That is my mentality. So, it does not matter what I like for I know if I do what He likes, that I will start liking it. I started preaching when I did not want to, and now you could not stop me! I stayed in Alaska because He asked me to stay, and now you could not get me to leave.

It cannot ever matter what we feel, think or want, for He owns us and has a right to ask us to do anything. At the same time, He rarely makes demands. He only makes demands at a certain spiritual level. If we are talking to a three-year-old child, it would not make any sense to make a demand, for it would mean nothing to them. But we can make a demand on a thirteen-year-old for they know something else is coming. Christ our Lord will not make a demand on babies, instead He will just simply ask them. He has told me this many times, "You can do what you want, but if you want to be in My will, you will do what you are told." It is a spiritual language and we have to understand the Lord's ways of communicating to us.

Engrafted by His Love

Matthew 5:8
Blessed are the Pure in heart for they shall see God.

The Greek word for pure is *"kathros."* It has a root meaning to be free from mixture. As believers, one of the problems we have is a lack of compatibility with our King. He brought us as a wild olive branch into the Vine. If we were to take a plant that broke off and put it into water to re-root it, we find a couple of weeks later that the plant has died. All that water could not help it. In the same way, when someone takes an organ from someone else's body and they put it inside a different body, they want it to adapt to that body as if it were the one that it came from. That is called ingrafting. In the same way, the Lord takes us – a wild olive branch, and He engrafts us into Him, by His love.

He is pumping love into our heart trying to get us to engraft His Word into our soul. Grace is doing in our heart what medicine does to that organ that does not belong in that foreign body. Grace, God's undeserved favor, ability and power is there to extend mercy to us because we are not capable of doing it for ourselves. If we do not do our part, eventually, that truth will be stolen according to scripture. But God's desire and hope is that we get rooted in Him and grow up so there is no more mixture – until our character is compatible with His. God's objective is to allow the Holy Spirit to build a foundation on the inside of us, for when we are talking about purity, motive is everything. It has to do with the reason as to why we do things or how we act a certain way when we do it.

The word pure is also a ceremonial word. It speaks of a heart that is laid out upon the altar for the inspection of God. This cleaning is spoken of in Psalm 139.

> **Psalm 139:23-24**
> Search me, O God, and know my heart: try me, and know my thoughts: And see if there be any wicked way in me, and lead me in the way everlasting.

We must open our hearts before the Lord and allow Him to inspect them to see if there is any impurity in our lives. If there is, we must allow Him to purify us. In Philippians 4:8, it uses the word pure, but it is a different Greek word than what is used in Matthew 5:8. It is *"dikaios"* and it means to be: equitable in character or act. The Fruit of the Spirit is the character of God and to get that character, one must become pure in heart. There are stumbling blocks that must be removed to produce equitable character – innocent, just, meek and what is upright and righteous in our lives. Therefore God allows tests and trials, basically they search out in you and bring to surface stuff you don't even know that's there. This is what David is saying in this verse.

Stream of Purity

> **Philippians 4:8**
> Finally, brethren, whatsoever things are true, what-soever things are honest, whatsoever things are just, whatsoever things are pure, whatsoever things are

lovely, whatsoever things are of good report, if there
by any virtue, if there be any praise, think on these
things.

The purity that is referenced to in Matthew 5:8 is purity at its
essence or core. It deals with the root from which can spring
forth purity. The root for purity that is found in Philippians
4:8 means before we can have a stream of purity in our lives,
we have to have a source from where it flows.

In the early 1800s there was a dead animal that fell into a
stream, which polluted the river and the villager's source of
water, causing a plague to come that destroyed the villages.
Even though the stream was pure to begin with, something
got into the stream and polluted it. So we have to make sure
that we keep the pollution out of the stream or river that flows
from the core of our being. That is why we are told to focus
on: whatsoever things are pure, whatsoever things are lovely,
whatsoever things are just. We need to keep our stream pure
and not pollute it with something that does not belong in it.

Proverbs 22:11

He that loveth pureness of heart, for the grace of
his lips the king shall be his friend.

Once we understand pureness of heart, we will only desire it,
because from it will determine our motives and why we do
what we do. *"He that loveth pureness of heart, for the grace of
his lips the king shall be his friend."* What will cause the King to
want to draw near to us? Compatibility. When our character
becomes like His, for the core of what we are comes from,
Christ our Lord who is the source. Remember, one of the

processes for purifying our soul is when we receive revelation from meditating on the Word of God. When we do and then seek an answer from Him, what He speaks will be a pure answer. Then we in turn must speak that truth into our heart that will impact our motive and attitude.

The Old Testament use of the word pure has the same meaning as Matthew 5:8. Yet, the meaning of the word heart is difficult to describe because often in the Old Testament the word heart is talking about the soul. But sometimes it is talking about the spirit, because the spirit man could not be changed in the Old Testament. What God was dealing with under the Old Testament was the soul. In other words, one must make a decision because God could not clean the heart of man under the Old Covenant. Or another way to say it, God could not purify the source under the Old Covenant. So, purity has to do with our inner desires and motives. It incorporates the soul or the activities of our mind, will and emotions. In Old Testament times it was the inner motivating source of their lives.

Matthew 6:21

For where your treasure is there will your heart be also.

Our treasure does not necessarily have to be money. It is what we believe in and put our trust in, either we put our trust in the carnal life or in the Kingdom of God. I always say, we are going to do what we believe, and if we do not change what we believe – if it is in error, we can forget about changing our motives. What we believe becomes our treasures.

81

Source of Purity

Matthew 15:8

These people draw nigh unto Me with their mouth and honor Me with their lips, but their heart is far from Me.

Under the Old Testament that was all that they could do was honor Him with their mouths. The source – their hearts, was still corrupt. So, they had to act out what they were saying with their lips to curtail what they were doing. This is why God put so many symbolisms throughout the Old Testament and instructed them to follow so many protocols. In order to habitually turn them back to Him, because their hearts – the source, were corrupt. He could not purify them the same way that He can with us today. He wrote His commandment on our hearts. The Source is not corrupt, but it is getting polluted in our souls downstream. This is what we have to work on, or we will have a bad house; a house that will not stand in difficult times. If our foundation is not pure, our house will crumble.

Matthew 12:34

O generation of vipers, how can ye, being evil, speak good things? for out of the abundance of the heart the mouth speaketh.

In Christ our Lord' time, viper was like a foul word or fighting word that He spoke to the people. That is why they killed Him. *"O generation of vipers, how can ye being evil* – the source, *speak good things?"* They could not because the source was corrupt. *"For out of the abundance of the heart the mouth speaketh."* So, the mouth is the bank of our river. You may want to ask yourself, who is fishing at your bank? Whose report are you believing? If our bank is polluted, we need to stop fishing there and go fish at somebody else's bank that is pure. Meaning, start listening to somebody else, for we are the last person that we need to listen to because we need to change what we are hearing, so we can change what we believe. Then our actions and motives will be pure.

A Good Man's Stream is Clean

Christ our Lord goes on to say in Matthew 12:35 that a good man's stream is clean. In other words, the bank of his river does not have weeds and litter all around it. And from his heart comes good treasures that will bring forth good things. But an evil man, whether Christian or non-Christian, is based upon what is coming out of their heart. Even though our Source is clean, we are letting our words pollute our stream because our mind is not renewed. So, what we believe and where we put our trust, will bring forth evil treasures, or bad fruit in our lives.

One of the clearest revelations of a person or who they truly are is evident by how they speak. Open your mouth and it will not take long before I can locate you. Why? Because whatever is overwhelming a person's heart at the time they speak, out of the abundance of their heart their mouth speaks. whatever is knocking at the door of your heart through your mind, whether words or circumstances do not let it get into your heart in abundance. The reason I know it is in a person's heart is because it did not get filtered out through the filter of Philippians 4:8.

83

Philippians 4:8

Finally, brethren, whatsoever things are true, whatsoever things are honest, whatsoever things are just, whatsoever things are pure, whatsoever things are lovely, whatsoever things are of good report, if there by any virtue, if there be any praise, think on these things.

Our filter is part of our foundation and if we are believing the wrong things, then we are filtering with a dirty filter. Again, what is the major problem with a tainted filter? We will believe the wrong thing. And if we do not change what we believe, we cannot change our filter because our filter affects our imagination; what we see and how we see it.

Everybody else does not see it. But we see it, because our filter is tainted, and it is affecting our imagination and our judgment. It will affect every part of our lives. It will eventually start to affect our body. The purity of heart goes to the very core of who we are because actions precede from motives. What am I saying? If our motives are pure, we will see God.

He is Love and He is Light

This brings us back to who God is. Two things describe the essence of God according to 1 John 1:5 and 4:8. He is love and He is light and within those elements is His life. This is what determines our Father's character and it is why we know He is good. His thoughts toward us, which determines His motives toward us, are good. If our motives are not right, then there is mixture in us, therefore; we are walking in darkness. Again, the Source is pure but we have polluted the waters.

> **1 John 4:16**
> And we have known and believed the love God had to us. God is love. And he that dwelleth in love, dwelleth in God and God in him.

Everything goes back to love. We can only dwell in love by obeying Him, both the written Word and the rhema words that He gives to instruct our steps. When we obey, we walk in light, as He is light. God is light because He is love. If we walk in love, we will keep the light on inside of us, even though there are still occasions for stumbling, the light is always present. There will be a constant flow of revelation telling us where to step and what the enemy is trying to do. The enemy cannot pull the wool over our eyes. Love will keep mixture out of our soul and keep our stream pure. If it is true but not lovely, we will not think about it because of love flowing through us. We will think the best of everybody, even if they prove we should not, we will still constantly try to think the best of them. So, as we become more and more perfected in love, we emulate and release more light. As the light of His glory becomes a part of us, it will make our heart pure. This is what ensures that the good fruit of the garden of our heart grows and matures. This is why love is the first responder, the one that shows up first, for it feeds those around it.

Stepping out of love is not just refraining from doing acts of love, or being nice. When we refrain from walking in love, it is not doing what God says. The first definition of love can be defined when Christ our Lord said, *"If you love Me, then obey Me."* We are to do what He says. If we do what He says, then our motives will be one of love, therefore; purity of heart has to do with our innermost motivations. When our motivations become that of heaven's love, our heart becomes pure. We grow not just by doing it because He says so, but because we love Him and love what and who He loves, which is people.

So, ask yourself a question. Why do you do what you do? Everything is a process. We must pray and ask the Lord to establish us in love which is the bond of perfection. Love is the glue that holds everything together and enables us to grow and bring forth abundant, everlasting good fruit for His Kingdom.

Motivated by Love

1 John 4:16
And we have known and believed the love God had to us. God is love. And he that dwelleth in love, dwelleth in God and God in him.

Let me say it a different way; he that chooses to act or be motivated by love, dwelleth in love or dwelleth in God. When we think the best about others, God is directly wanting to affect our motive. So, we must choose to act in love at all times. We cannot talk about purity without talking about love. Because it is love that purifies us. So as we walk in love, it pours through us and begins to purify us. Equally, wherever love goes, it floods us with light and revelation showing us more and more of who Christ our Lord really is. If there is light, then there is wisdom. Christ Our Lord was made unto us wisdom, righteousness, sanctification and redemption. So, we must ask the Lord to fill us with His love. But remember, it can only manifest when we do what He says, all the time!

So, our quest should be in every given opportunity, how can we manifest love. I know that is a challenge when some people deservingly need to be kicked into the middle of next week. But that is what the overcoming life is all about. That is why we are called overcomers; we must overcome ourselves. The challenge is to constantly deal with things of the past that manifests itself in our future. Someone betrayed us and we reacted to them with anger. It is a mark on our past that tainted our soul and we act today like it is going to happen again, so we have very little trust in people. To be free we must choose to love and forgive everybody. This is the road to perfection.

> **John 15:12-14** (*KJV*)
> This is my commandment, That ye love one another, as I have loved you. Greater love hath no man than this, that a man lay down his life for his friends. Ye are my friends, if ye do whatsoever I command you.

Christ our Lord would forgive us if we sinned against Him 499 times in one day and more, that means we have too as well. So why do we keep telling people that a person is getting on our nerves? What if God said that to us? Remember the parable Christ Our Lord gave about the guy who would not forgive the one that owed him a few dollars, yet He forgave him millions of dollars. If we do not learn to walk in forgiveness, we will be turned over to the tormentors. God is saying, "If we will not humble ourselves, then I will bring along some people or situations to help humble you. I am going to turn you over to the tormentor." Well, the tormentor is the devil and we might end up dying in prison.

Verse 13 says, *"Greater love hath no man than this, that he lay down his life for his friends."* Every time we make a decision to do what He says, we lay down our lives. We are putting aside what we want and doing what He wants. There is no greater love than that. We keep our opinions to ourselves when we do what He says. That is the greatest death that we can die. This is the life of the overcomer. We are not doing what actions dictate, instead we are motivated by love.

If we walk in the Spirit, the Holy Spirit will show us why someone does what they do. But if He does not, do not judge the heart. We do not know what makes a person tick. The Lord is the only One that does but if we are His friend, He will come and whisper in our ear and share their heart's motive and tell us this is why we need to pray for them. Then mercy and pity will flow and we will pray for them as if it were for our own broken soul. That is compassion that love produces.

Love is Cheap without Action

Verse 14 says, you are my friend, IF you do whatever I command you. His command is that we love each other and pray for those who persecute and despitefully use us. That means more than saying, "I love you." Love is cheap without any action attached to it. His Word says, faith without works is dead.

Verse 15 says, if you do this henceforth, I call you not servants. There is a relationship change that happens when one dies to self and walks in love. Many people in heaven who dwell in the outer court were His servants and they simply did what He said. But their motives were wrong even when they did it.

They had some ulterior motive. Some had something to gain behind it that was carnal in nature. It was not because they loved Him. If we love Him and do it because we love Him, He will flood us with His emotions and feelings for a person or situation. And we will do what He is asking with His feelings and emotions and begin to become One with Him, spirit, soul and body. *"I call you not servants, for the servant knoweth not what His Lord doeth, but I call you friends; for all things I heard of my Father I have made known unto you"*(John 15:15).

If we become a friend of Christ our Lord by walking in love, by obeying Him unto death if that is what He requires of us, He is saying that He will share His secrets with us. He will tell us what He is doing and why. That is why God the Father will not tell Christ our Lord when He is coming, because He will tell us, His friends.

Proverbs 22:11

He that loveth pureness of heart for the grace of his lips the King shall be His friend.

Solomon got that revelation even before Christ Our Lord spoke, *"Blessed are the pure in heart for they shall see God."* The words "see God" have a number of meanings. The prime meaning is to literally see Him. That is my quest before I leave this earth, but I also want to continue to see Him with an unveiled face. Unveiling happens when revelation comes, and we will also see what He wants us to see. Whether it be something concerning ourselves or something concerning Him. Whether it be something concerning the Father or something concerning the future. It will be something that we need at that moment and time, but the prime meaning is to see God. The Greek word is *"optomai."* It is used in a certain tense and means: to see with both eyes wide open. That can be that our conscious mind is aware of what our spiritual eyes are seeing in that moment. It also means: something remarkable and different from which denotes simple voluntary observation which expresses merely mechanical, passive or casual through a vision yet still more emphatically in its tense. It signifies a more continued inspection. It is a watching from a distance: to appear, look, see or show.

Seated in Heavenly Places

Most Christians have a bad habit that when we do not understand something in the scriptures, we spiritualize it. Theologians do it often by saying it is just a metaphor. Christ Our Lord said, *"If you have seen Me, you have seen the Father."* Sadly, many Christians do not think that they can see the Lord, today on this earth literally, or the Father for that matter. The spirit realm is accessible to every born-again believer. For we are seated with Him in heavenly places, but we have to believe that He says what He means and means what He says all the time. That is what the Bible says and that He will walk and talk with us from that realm, as He walked with Adam and Eve. The transitional relationship: from servant to friend. He wants to stop giving you orders and come sit beside you and say, "Would you do this for Me?" Why does He want to come to us this way? Because He knows we will not turn Him down as friend.

2 Timothy 4:22

The Lord Jesus Christ be with thy spirit. Grace be

with you. Amen.

Do not spiritualize that He wants to be your friend and walk with you in intimate fellowship. Sometimes He will come and pull you away, whether your soul or spirit inside your garden which is on the inside of you. You will be literally walking with Him inside of the garden that you and the Holy Spirit are building for Him. Did not He say, *"I will dwell in them; I will walk in them. I will be their God; they will be my people."* This is a deeper revelation of that scripture where He will come and pull you inside of this garden, which is in the center of your belly, and you will be sitting there with Him in your garden.

Our garden is purified based on the level of truth and love that we have walked in. I encourage you to invite Him there when you meditate upon Him. It is one thing for Him to come in a vision and it is another thing for Him to show up inside of you, which He likes to do and have fellowship with you. But not as Master and servant, but walking in your garden and sitting beside you and talking to you as friend.

So how do we become friends with an invisible Spirit? That is the challenge. We are an invisible spirit as well that has never seen the real us. Our spirit dwells in the eternal realm. So, we have to learn to enter into His realm – the realm of the Spirit, where He is the door. The more our veils are removed, the more our soul is restored and the quicker that will happen on a regular basis. Scientists today talk about parallel universes. Every movie that comes out now talks about parallel universes. Really universe is the wrong word to use. Because when we think about the universe, we think of galaxies when it actually should be realms. They say we occupy the same space with another world. It is true of the spirit realm. The spirit realm wraps around this realm. The spirit realm gave birth to this earthly realm; the seeing realm.

All God has to do is drop the veils from our eyes and we will see everything in the spirit realm around us. That is why that realm is dangerous to many Christians. As we pray and worship, we enter into His gates or through the door which He Himself is into His presence or spirit realm. Many times, unbeknown to our conscious mind we enter into that realm. We are spirit, mind and body and the part of us that is spirit, and even our soul, can travel into heaven – into that realm, unbeknown to the rest our soul and body. Did not Isaiah say, *"I will mount up with wings as eagles?"* Beloved, that is literal because the soul has wings and different layers.

I Write unto You a New Commandment

1 John 2:8-9

Again, a new commandment I write unto you which things are true in Him and you because the darkness has passed and the true light now shineth. He that saith that he is in the light and hates his brother is in darkness even until now.

John is saying as a child of the light that we pollute the stream that flows out of us when we walk in hatred or unforgiveness. For he who says he is in the light but hates his brother is in darkness.

1 John 2:10

He that loveth his brother abideth in the light, and there is none occasion of stumbling in him.

92

When we walk in love, His light increases within us and the devil cannot pull the wool over our eyes. He cannot because everywhere we look, there is light preventing us from stumbling!

1 John 4:7-8

Beloved, let us love one another: for love is God; and everyone that loveth is born of God, and knoweth God. He that loveth not knoweth not Go; for God is love.

So, purity of heart has to do with motive, why we do something. And the root of that motive, if we are to be pure in heart and see God, will be love. "Blessed are the pure in heart for they shall see God." We will see God as he is, even through the light that he clothed himself with. We will also see him in everything just as the cherubim spoke about in Isaiah 6:3, The whole earth is full of His glory!

* * *

Chapter 7: Blessed Are The Peacemakers

Matthew 5:9

Blessed are the peacemakers: for they shall be called the children of God.

The anti-Christ spirit is active in America because of the lack of peace in the Church. I am not saying there will be hostility, mostly likely there will be, but when we do not walk in truth there is no peace. When Christ Our Lord was brought before Pilate, the religious leaders and all in the crowd that had gathered could not come to a consensus of what He was guilty of doing. All the witness's stories did not collaborate. There was no peace amongst them because they did not believe in the truth that was right in front of them. Pilot asked the question, "What is truth?" He was looking at truth and because of the warning from his wife, who had a dream about this righteous Man, it brought the fear of the Lord upon him that caused him to struggle to release Christ our Lord but he could find no peace. They wanted His blood and Christ our Lord surrendered His life, but He did not surrender His peace. For He would have not been able to do what He did if He lost His peace.

How did Christ Our Lord maintain His peace? In the Garden of Gethsemane, He said, *"O My Father, if it is possible, let this cup pass from Me; nevertheless, not as I will, but as You will."* It was not death that He was afraid of, it was separation from the peace – the presence of the Father God that caused Him to fear. Most do not understand that struggle that He faced. The unbeliever does not understand that because even though they do not know Christ our Lord, they still sense the peace and presence of God, as His Spirit is everywhere. Those who end up in hell are in 24-hour horror, because they cannot feel, sense, know or see the presence of peace: God.

There are different levels of peace that we experience, such as the peace that came inside of us at our new birth, where it manifested as one of the Fruits of the Spirit. However, as that fruit grows, we should be depositing that peace through the truth that we release everywhere we go, making peace between God and man, as they accept the Prince of Peace into their hearts. But there is also a lower level of that peace that will manifest wherever there is disharmony, where we bring peace by the wisdom that we speak to make enemies into friends.

River of Peace

We need to understand, Christ our Lord is serious about duplicating and growing that peace inside of us. We must have it, if we are to successfully navigate through the last days that are upon us. One of the foundational truths that must flow through our lives, just like the river that flows from the throne of God, is peace. Peace is being taken from the earth and the peacemaker must arise inside of us. It is interesting that in all of the doctrine of the Beatitudes, one of the truths that is put forth is the culmination of that truth; meaning when we are a doer of something this is what we become. For example, *"Blessed are the pure in heart for they shall see God."* The more God can remove the veil that is over the eyes of our heart's or understanding, the clearer we can see, for when that happens it restores our soul.

When our soul is darkened by things of the past, it is like wearing glasses with scratches on the lenses. We take them to the eye doctor, telling him that we need new ones because we cannot see out of them. The doctor then cleans them with his special tools making them like new. We think we have new glasses, but instead he just cleaned them. This is what God is doing with our soul, with the end result that we would be able to see God. This is literally, not figuratively. Remember, our soul wraps around our spirit and our spirit sees through the contamination that is in our soul.

Peace is Sonship Status

So interestingly enough, the Author tells us that the culmination of being a person of peace will bring us into sonship. Of all the character traits and the foundational principles, this is the one that gives us the stature and the character of the Son. Christ Our Lord came to break down the wall of division and enmity between God and man. He was called by the angels: The Prince of Peace. Peace is an honor that comes from God and upon a person like a cloak or knighthood. When we are carrying that for the King, we represent Him in a way where we can speak for Him; where we can release things for Him. It is a sonship stature.

For instance, recently, Queen Elizabeth announced that not Prince Charles, but his son would come into the kingship. Though he is a young man and has not stepped into that office as yet, all the honor, stature and glory of kingship is on this young man. And now he is being groomed as such. We need to understand, this is what the enemy sees in the realm of the spirit, even though he knows that we have not attained it or earned it, he is not going to respect it. Every day of our lives he will do what it takes to see to it that we do not step into our kingly role. Even though according to the Word it is already reckon to us. That means by faith, we can walk in the power of it even though it is not fully formed in us yet. That is not fronting, that is faith!

The Bible says, let the weak say I am strong. When we say it and the devil sees in the spirit our weakness and not our strongness, he runs up against it, but he ends up running against the grace that we have been given and that is what makes the difference. That is the principle of the Kingdom, as we fight in faith, peace is being formed within us. Verse nine indicates a peacemaker is a person who has obtained a certain level of maturity in God. The term: son of God is used to describe a person who has become a mature son of God. Christ Our Lord is telling us that on our road to sonship we cannot abandon our duties as a peacemaker or we will not get there.

Mature Sons of God

The Greek word for son is *"huios."* It means a fully matured son. I have five boys and when people speak of them, they call them my sons. There was a day they were not fully matured sons, but they grew up to become men. The scripture calls us sons of God and that includes both male and female for He is not speaking about gender, but about a spiritual status that we are to obtain in Him. This is what God desires and needs more than anything else to come forth from His Remnant in these last days.

The state of Alaska could be described as a hunting person's paradise. No farther in his right mind would give his shotgun to his ten-year old son and tell him to go out and learn how to shoot. Instead, he will take him to the woods and thoroughly teach him the safety rules and how to clean the rifle. This is what God is trying to do with us, but most of His children want to stay children. They do not want to grow up. If we do not want to grow up, then the end result will be paradise in heaven, which is also known as the outer-court. It is the largest habitation realm for saints in heaven. It is where most

Christians end up when they die, because they did not mature in their walk on this earth.

Just like God tried His best to get Israel into the Promised Land, but they insisted in walking in their unbelief, murmuring and disobedience to His ways. Therefore, only two – Joshua and Caleb, entered into the fullness of their inheritance because spiritually the rest of them would not mature; they would not listen to Him. So, He had to discard them, and wait for their children. This is exactly what is happening to the Church today. This is where we are now in God's time frame. Most of the children of God that He will use to bring peace to this earth is the Millennials.

When God said of Christ our Lord, "This is My Son." Everyone who heard this knew what it meant. It referred to the Jewish custom of placing a son into his father's business – or trade. Romans chapter five talks about the adoption of children that we go through as a believer.

Matthew 3:17

And lo a voice from heaven saying, This is my beloved Son, in whom I am well pleased.

In an Orthodox Jewish household, the father never calls his male children's sons, until they reach the age of 30. During a boy's Bar Mitzvah, at the age of 13-years-old, he enters the training hood of sonship under the watchful eye of the father. So, in essence, the Father was saying about His Son – Christ Our Lord, to all those who were present that He has reached maturity. He is ready to represent the family and carry My name as peacemaker. Only a person full of His peace can deliver that peace to those who are enemies of the Cross. This is the kind of person Christ Our Lord is talking about in Matthew 5:9.

The peacemaker becomes a mature son, when he releases what the Father is giving to him. A peacemaker is one who has totally surrendered their attitudes and motives to the Father and have only one agenda – His agenda, in all that they do. Christ Our Lord surrendered all to the Father, therefore; He knows His ways and heart for all people and all situations. At the same time, He is putting the finishing touches on those He is calling peacemakers in this final hour. Those who are willing to surrender all to Him, will bring peace everywhere they go. God is not interested in establishing a Kingdom physically here on this earth, not yet anyway. He first wants to establish His Kingdom on the inside of us so that it can be displayed all around us. Our responsibility is to bring peace to the lives of people where there is turmoil. When we do, we are bringing the Kingdom of God, inside of people's lives.

Christ our Lord is speaking about laying a foundation of character in one's life. And to reach this status of peacemaker, prosperity and rest must be a part of our lives. People are troubled and full of fear about many changes in society and their life. The number one pill that doctors are prescribing today is for anxiety. That is the inability to maintain mental control. The reason that is increasing is because of the level of darkness that is being released in the land. And we are to be the peacemaker – the answer, to that darkness. Mark 16 says one of our responsibilities is to cast out devils, if we are to bring peace into troubled lives. For it is demons that disrupts a person's peace.

Due to our sins, there was a dividing wall between us and God, which the Lord broke down by His death upon the Cross.

We should seek to be peacemakers and break down the walls of partition and division between friends, husbands and wives, children and parents, churches and ministries. There is also a wall that He is endeavoring to remove between our soul and spirit called the veil, so that our spirit, soul and body might become one.

Ephesians 2:14

For he is our peace, who hath made both one, and hath broken down the middle wall of partition between us.

As the seventh beatitude flows out from the sixth beatitude, it pronounces a blessing upon the peacemaker. As believers, we should seek to bring reconciliation in the Body of Christ for we are the most divided unit of people on the planet.

A Peace Offering

Leviticus 3:1-5

And if his oblation be a sacrifice of peace offering, if he offer it of the herd; whether it be a male or female, he shall offer it without blemish before the Lord.2 And he shall lay his hand upon the head of his offering, and kill it at the door of the tabernacle of the congregation: and Aaron's sons the priests shall sprinkle the blood upon the altar round about.3 And he shall offer of the sacrifice of the peace offering an offering made by fire unto the Lord; the fat that covereth the inwards, and all the fat that is upon the inwards,4 And the two kidneys, and the fat that is on them, which is by the flanks, and the caul above the liver, with the kidneys, it shall he take away.**5** And Aaron's sons shall burn it on the altar upon the burnt sacrifice, which is upon the wood that is on the fire: it is an offering made by fire, of a sweet savour unto the Lord.

This describes what an Israelite had to do in order to have peace. An offering had to be brought to the Lord. This involved sacrifice on the part of the person bringing the offering; it cost him something. That is why David said he would not give to God that which cost him nothing. We have Christians all the time who do not want to do something that will cost them a price. If it costs them something, they do not want to do it.

We see from these verses that it was to be an offering made by fire unto the Lord, and that it was to be without blemishes or imperfections. That the person was to lay his hands upon the head of the offering and kill it at the door of the Tabernacle. Then the priest was to sprinkle the blood upon the altar, and offer the sacrifice as a peace offering – an offering made by fire unto the Lord. The priest was to remove the fat that covered the inwards, the two kidneys and the fat that was upon them, and the caul above the liver. And then burn it on the altar upon the burnt sacrifice that was upon the wood that was on the fire. Remember, everything God does has a purpose.

Look at the two main ingredients used in the offering. The fat of the animal and the kidneys. The picture is very interesting. Fat, symbolically speaks of strength. If we were to take away the fat in our bodies, typically around our joints, it would cause us to lose a lot of strength.

Seat of our Emotions

The kidney is another story. The kidneys are an unusual symbolic picture depicting the controlling element of our lives. This word, kidney, goes back to the Hebrew concept of the heart. Which today, we know that the heart controls everything because it is what causes the blood to flow throughout our bodies – without a heartbeat we would die. The kidneys were regarded by the early Hebrews as the seat of the emotions. When an angel came to me many years ago and stuck his hand into me, that is where he stuck it, into the seat of my emotions. The Bible translators had real trouble in translating this word into a meaningful English word. They finally came up with the English word "reins." That is what they used in the translation, substituting the word "kidneys" for "reins." They felt this made the meaning clearer, but in actuality they really damaged it, because when we look at it, it does not mean anything to us.

Psalm 7:9

Oh let the wickedness of the wicked come to an end; but establish the just: for the righteous God trieth the hearts and reins.

Where it says, *"God trieth the heart and the reins,"* it actually should say, *"God trieth the heart and the kidneys."* It does not make sense though – what is God doing with our kidneys? The translators could not bring themselves to translate it as the Lord did. It sounds like the Lord is trying to make you pee! So, they changed it, causing it not to convey the real meaning of the concept of the word, which is our seat of emotions.

103

Psalms 139:13

For thou have possessed my reins.

What does God want with our kidney's? Reins are like the reins on a horse, so they figure it was the same concept, controlling a horse with the reins. "Thy has covered me in my mother's womb." So, if we see the word kidney it makes more sense, right? The same word is carried over into the New Testament.

Revelation 2:23

And I will kill her children with death; and all the churches shall know that I am He which searches the reins and hearts. And I will give unto every one of you according to your works.

Where they have used the word reins, it should be the word kidneys.

Handing Over the Reins of our Lives

The word kidneys used in the peace offering represents human desires; man's will. Or, the controlling factor in one's life. It speaks to why we do what we do – our motives. This is why God so desperately wants to restore our soul. Remember, I used the analogy of a horse controlled with reins. So that part of our lives has to be offered to the Lord. It is a peace offering to Him. We have to bring it to Him willingly, for He will not take it from us.

So, what am I saying? To have peace, we have to hand over the reins of our lives to the Lord. Many in the Church are not developing in peace, which is a Fruit of the Spirit. But this is so much more. When peace flows as a river in our lives, we are not just established in it, but we are releasing it everywhere we go. The lack thereof will keep us out of the will of God and we will not be doing what God called us to do. We will not be what God created us to be. All of that is the reins of our lives.

Not knowing what we are called to do is not an excuse, because God has given us all the tools that we need to find out. He told us, *"That if you will draw near to Me, I will draw near to you. If you ask Me, I will answer you. I will respond to you."* He is always asking the question, *"Are you on the right channel or are you hearing what you want to hear?"* That is how it is with a lot of Christians, we often hear them say, *"That is not what I want to hear. I don't want to do that."* Some people think so much of themselves – of their life, of their call or their profession that they would not dare leave it up to God.

Remember, in order to have peace in our lives, we have to hand over the reins to God. The second ingredient of the peace offering was fat. As I said before, fat represents strength. The Israelites had to bring a sacrifice and offer the kidneys or reins and the fat or strength. It takes a lot of fat – or strength, to hand over the kidneys, the reins of our lives. So, one of the aspects of the Kingdom of God is peace. And it will require a peace offering that we bring willingly to be burnt on the altar of sacrifice, if we are to obtain Sonship.

Romans 14:17

For the kingdom of God is not meat and drink; but righteousness, and peace, and joy in the Holy Ghost.

Why are we going to need so much joy in these coming days?

Because all of the death and dying that is going to be happening around us, we are going to have to be stabilized by the joy of the Lord. The joy of the Lord is going to return at such a level that it will start restoring our physical bodies. It will start renewing our youth as the eagle. The joy of the Lord will bring the strength that we need to do what He is asking – His strength, and in return that strength will cause us to walk in peace. We will need the peace of God upon us even when we are to decree death to an entire village or to an entire city. We cannot do that without the presence of God. Or we will end up doing what King Saul did when he kept some alive and then blame the people for his disobedience. This was not the time to show compassion for God said he was to kill everything, and he did not.

The Pursuit of Peace

Psalms 34:14

Depart from evil and do good. Seek peace and pursue it.

We are told to pursue peace, but in John 15:9 we are told to abide in love. Brothers and sisters, we can only bring or minister to others what we have become ourselves. We must become peace before we can bring it to others. It is a character of God that is tangible to us in the natural realm. And as we die to ourselves, handing over the reins of our lives to God, we begin to enter into peace. Dying to oneself – our will, is the pursuit of peace. Do we care about what happens to us? Do we care about what other people think of us? Do we care about what other people say about us? If we do, then Christ

Our Lord does not have control over our lives.

Once we enter this place in God, everything changes. Our whole outlook on life is transformed. It is no longer you that lives. The enemy does not know how to handle a person who has entered into peace because nothing can affect them. They cannot be bought. They cannot be sold. They are not a charlatan. They do not care about recognition or titles. The biggest problem in the Church today is the Babylonian spirit which is to make a name for one's self. Peacemakers do not care about who gets the credit. All they are interested in is that Christ our Lord be exalted, it matters not what happens to them. The only thing the devil can really do to a peacemaker is kill them! Amen!

That is what he did to the Apostles. We cannot be a peacemaker and love our lives. A peacemaker will be the most hated person on the planet and the most loved when they show up because they will bring His presence with them. God will always have different levels of light in the Kingdom. What He needs now more than ever is for sons to mature, for this is His objective for our lives. He cannot do it with babies – toddlers, because when they get tired of training, they have had enough and they go play.

If we want to enter the realm of heaven in our daily walk with the Lord, a realm of peace that passes all understanding, where nothing can disturb us, we must bring a peace offering to the Lord every day. In our walk with God, in our pursuit of God, we will come face to face in situations and circumstances and right in the midst of tests is where God shows us what we are really made of. In that place, He is asking us, *"Will you bring that to Me – all your fear, bitterness, shame, jealousy?"* That is a peace offering which has been a part of us for so long that it

107

has made us into who we are and He wants to take it from us and use it for our good. But our will – our flesh, is an enemy to the Cross and can be very hard to lay down. So we often say to the Lord sanctify it or use it, but God wants us to kill it and nail it to the Cross. He wants us to bring our peace offerings and lay them on the altar. When we do, that is pursuing peace by allowing God to devastate us – to break us, so that He can use us for His glory!

* * *

Chapter 8: Blessed Are The Persecuted

Matthew 5:10
　　Blessed are they that are persecuted for righteousness' sake: for theirs is the kingdom of heaven.

More than anything we need to know that the foundation
of the Lord stands sure in our life. Just as Christ our Lord
wears His scars on His back and the holes in His hand, we
need to know they speak of victory and not defeat. So too, is
it for us. Our persecution is the scars of victory, where the
martyrs' marks have brought death to our flesh – a death to
our will, in exchange for His will. Those marks will always
be upon our bodies bringing us rewards, as the result of them.
This is why the Lord tells us that we are blessed when we are
persecuted. We need to stop believing the lie that we are getting

the short end of the stick or that we are doing something wrong when we suffer. We are blessed when we are persecuted for righteousness' sake. Again, not just doing righteousness. That is a part of it, but by us simply being righteous, we face persecution.

As it gets darker, the enemy will be able to identify us easier because he can see not only our light in the spirit realm, but our threat level also. He knows our authority according to the brilliancy of that light. Hence, persecution. This is why persecution is going to increase and the Lord will allow it. We are the ones the enemy is going to attack the most. We need to understand Satan cannot cut off our light, we have to do that ourselves. We are the ones who have to put it under a bushel. We put it under a bushel by walking in unrighteousness, getting into strife, unforgiveness, fault finding and bickering, as some examples.

Qualifying us for Kingship

The shedding of innocent blood brings many souls into the Kingdom. This is one of the mysteries of the Cross. On the positive side, God promised that we would drink from the same cup of suffering as Christ Our Lord did. It is another great mystery how God uses our pain and suffering to qualify us for Kingship. Most in the Church do not understand this mystery. They think that the more they are persecuted, the more it denotes failure in their lives. That the longer it takes to get what they want by faith, the more it promotes failure, which is a lie. If we walk any length of time with Jehovah sneaky, I am going to tell you He loves waiting until the last minute to do things or to bring the breakthrough we need. He loves it because He has an objective, for He is the Master Teacher! All our severe tests and trials are ultimately getting us ready for why we are here on planet earth, that we may fulfill our purpose.

Many brothers and sisters have died prematurely because they would not allow God to take them through the valley of the shadow of death, that is lined with persecution. God brings some people into our lives to release persecution upon us so that He can judge them. That is a principle of the Kingdom. We see God did that with Pharaoh. He also said when the cup of the Amorites is full, that He was going to bring judgment upon them. Some people deserve judgment and even death. So, God brings certain people into our lives to purposely mistreat us so that He can judge them down the road. That is the righteousness of God. And, only God knows if they will humble themselves temporarily like Pharaoh and then harden their hearts again. Or, if they will truly humble themselves, which will cause God's grace and righteousness to be extended to them.

God's judgments will come to them, only if we have refused to retaliate against them in the spirit realm. It is possible to retaliate against others in the Spirit, but not retaliate physically against them. For example; if our thoughts toward someone are not good but evil, we end up releasing spells against them in the spirit realm. This is not good, or what we should be doing, for now we are fighting against the will of God for their life and our own lives. Especially, if God brought them into our lives in order to bring righteousness to them or to give them an opportunity to get it right with the Lord.

We are to be living Epistles that some are to read. Some

111

people will only get the opportunity to get right by reading our lives. By seeing how we respond to the evil that comes forth from their hearts towards us. Hence, the mystery of suffering. That is why we are blessed when we lay down our lives, when we do not take the opportunity to retaliate in word, action or thought life towards others. We may not be exalted now, but we will be later. We may not appear to be blessed now, but the blessing of God will overtake us later. Not just in things but in glory. Remember, Paul listed all the dreadful things that happen to him and called them light afflictions!

Our Light Afflictions

2 Corinthians 4:17-18

For our light affliction, which is but for a moment, worketh for us a far more exceeding and eternal weight of glory; **18** While we look not at the things which are seen, but at the things which are not seen: for the things which are seen are temporal; but the things which are not seen are eternal.

The path of persecution, endured in this world through suffering and obedience to the King, causes the love of God to abound in us bringing a level of purity and light that can outshine the stars in heaven. This is the road to perfection. It is the narrow road and why so few travel upon it. It is so narrow because it is marked with great sufferings along the way. People do not like to suffer for the King. If at any time Christ our Lord had retaliated for all that was done to Him, we would not be here today. But even as He hung on the Cross, He cried out, *"Father forgive them for they do not know what they are doing."* Let me show you a mystery, the bible says he went beyond the veil that is his flesh. His flesh became sin for us and at his death he went beyond it into that realm for us. When the soldier pierced him in his side, he pierced his veil which was his flush and into the most holy place.

In the same way when we are born again there is still a quality of darkness in all our souls, therefore James said the soul must be saved or restored. Restored how? Back to what the father originally intended, where he can abide within our soul and rule there. This is a process my dear brothers and sisters, it is called the process of the overcomer. When you overcome sin in the flesh, in doing so you become like him. So as you do the veil that your flesh produces in the realm of the spirit is based upon the purity of your soul or the lack thereof. The more love purifies you the more that veil disappears or the thinner it gets. Until it is totally removed, and you can walk in both realms at once. This is the life the Adam once had, and it was also the life the second Adam had.

There was a lady that the Lord came to and took her back in time. She could feel the wind blowing hard against her skin as she asked the Lord what was happening. The Lord told her, *"We are going back in time."* Then all of a sudden, they were standing at the foot of the Cross seeing the Lord disfigured beyond recognition, covered in His own blood. She said all during the Crucifixion every time they hit or stabbed the Lord, that He only saw the Father God the whole time. He would see the Father God would rise up from His throne like He was going to strike those who were crucifying His Son, but every time Christ our Lord would cry out, *"Father, forgive them."* Then the Father would sit back down.

Christ our Lord did not just say it on the Cross, but throughout the entire time of His crucifixion. Then Christ Our Lord would walk a little further and somebody would hit Him or do something and Father God would stand up again ready to strike. And Christ Our Lord would say, *"Father, forgive them."* And He would sit back down. This went on through the entire crucifixion. The Father was getting up to retaliate, but because of mercy that came from His Son, He stopped.

Brothers and Sisters, it is no different for us. We can extend someone's judgment, or we can shorten it. If we get fed up, then many times God will get fed up. When we are talking about someone else's soul and life that we hold in our hands and we can determine if they make it or not, by how much we are willing to suffer for them. Is our suffering worth it? Or, is our feelings getting hurt worth someone missing hell?

This is the main reason that He left us here. He incorporated sufferings into our lives, wanting us to grow into perfection, until we have become like Him in our words, thoughts and deeds. We must take the same sufferings that He took and overcome them how He did, all the while feeling the same way about it as He did. We cannot retaliate in our mind. We must keep our thoughts pure towards those hurting us. At times, we can feel so overwhelmed and be full of anger at the injustices. When that happens, we need to go cry at the Lord's feet and His alone. He will always come and embrace us. Whether we see Him, feel Him or not. He will always come.

I remember many times being hurt in the stuff that I went through. Even in the Church that I used to attend. The persecution that I went through. Many times, the Lord would come and cry with me because I was hurt. Within myself, after I finished crying and encouraged myself in the Lord. I got right back into the battle. Many times, what we think is not the battle is actually the battle that we are to overcome. In other words, what we think – the little things, as not important, are very important to heaven.

Enduring Mistreatment from Others

As believers, we must endure the mistreatment from others without reacting in an ungodly way. Even as Christ acted out the nature of the Lamb on the Cross, and not that of a lion, so should we endure persecution with a right and humble attitude. We will be persecuted because we follow Him.

> ### John 15:18-19
> If the world hate you, ye know that it hated me before it hated you. **19** If ye were of the world, the world would love his own: but because ye are not of the world, but I have chosen you out of the world, therefore the world hateth you.

If the world loves us, then we need to stop and ask ourselves if we are living a godly life. The world will hate us simply because we are good. And if we are good, we cannot stop doing good deeds; therefore, people will want to persecute us. Remember, it is about building our character to match His divine character and nature.

> ### 2 Timothy 3:12
> Yea, and all that will live godly in Christ Jesus shall suffer persecution.

If we seek to live a godly life, we can be sure that we will be persecuted. A dear young man said to his pastor, "I do not believe in Satan and I have never been troubled by him." The pastor, who was elderly, said, "I suppose you have never tried to live holy either. Of course, the enemy will not trouble you if you are not making waves and you will not be aware of him because you are walking in step with him. He will not trouble you for you are no threat to him." The enemy seeks to persecute those whom he knows are a great threat to the kingdom of darkness

Remember in the Beatitudes, they always had the end results to bless us. In this case with Matthew 5:10, there is a negative side and a positive side. *"Blessed are those who are persecuted."* But what is the end result if we go through persecution His way? *"Theirs is the Kingdom of heaven."* Kingdom speaks of that place of authority we are called to execute on this earth as it is in heaven. Brothers and Sisters, nothing can get us to that place more quickly than being persecuted, because of righteousness. I am not talking about getting into heaven, I am talking about being seated with Him in heavenly places. Seated with Him on His throne ruling and reigning with Him, pushing back the darkness that wants to destroy our purpose on this earth.

Matthew 5:11

Blessed are ye, when men shall revile you, and persecute you, and shall say all manner of evil against you falsely, for my sake.

When we are being persecuted, we want to make sure it is a false accusation against us, because if it is not, we will lose the blessedness. When it is a true persecution towards righteousness or us doing something right, something is being added to us spiritually when we are under attack. But we have to keep telling ourselves what we are suffering through is not for nothing. Because the enemy will tell us that we do not have to put up with it. Listen, if we want what the Lord is offering, we must recognize when it is a legitimate test, for earth is the only place where sons are made. Our day is coming to shine as the stars in the heavens.

But we must walk as He walked, being slapped and spit on by the very people He created and by the ones who should love us the most, but do not. When Christ our Lord endured the Cross, that was not His time to shine, but to suffer. This is our time to suffer, as well. The blessedness that comes into our lives is to help us maintain while we are suffering. To help us know that we are not alone, and it is not for nothing. Everything is connected, as we are all connected, and what we are doing is not only blessing us but it is blessing our children and our children's children. Listen, if the curse falls to the third and fourth generation, then the blessedness can too. Our blessedness and obedience come right against the curse and can unravel the curse that is upon our children and grandchildren.

Stay Focus and Maintain

So, when they revile you, persecute you, say all manner of evil about you for His sake, not yours. What is He saying in this verse? That He cannot get His work accomplished through us, if we do not stay focused, if we do not maintain. If we do not yield to what He wants to do in and through us, then He has to get it done through someone else. Every one of us has a part in building His Kingdom. Every one of us has a ministry that has been given to us to steward, where He is the Head. He took His ministry and threw it into the Body, where everyone in the Body has a part to accomplish. There are members of the many parts of that Body all over the world.

Our abilities to rejoice and be glad when going through persecution increases this blessedness. When Christ Our Lord was telling the Father to forgive them, that was an aspect of Him rejoicing. Rejoicing is not always just shouting hallelujah. Rejoicing is when we continue in the faith and in what we are doing, despite the hardships we face. Many times, that allows the persecution to run its course. So, praying, shouting hallelujah or whatever we need to do to enforce the victory, then do it, so that we do not stop in the midst of the persecution.

James 1:4
But let patience have her perfect work, that ye may be perfect and entire, wanting nothing.

Tribulation worketh patience. It will jump start patience in our lives if we let it. Patience is needed to endure in tribulation, and perfection is not possible without it. If we do not go through the trial that is set before us, then we are not going to go through the next one. Because in gaining experience we can encourage someone else, as well as ourselves, because we went through the fire. God will not fail when we are in the middle of our trial, He will always come through and with everyone else going through it with Him. Every time we endure and come out the other side of our sufferings – our trials, His way, our ability to stand in the long-haul increases. Let me tell you a little mystery of enduring temptation, make your mind up that I am willing even to be a martyr for him. When you do you will be prepared for what lies ahead.

Some people fail so easily because they are not willing to go through suffering His way; they want an easy way out. Therefore, they do not let patience have its perfect work in the difficult situations in their lives. If we are to be of any use to the King, then we must suffer. I do not know why God chose this path for our lives. It is a mystery, but it is a key ingredient in creating Kings and Priests on this earth to accomplish His Kingdom plans in and through our lives. Just like we need ingredients to make a cake. If we leave certain parts out, it will come out of the oven brown, maybe a little flat and even edible, but it will not look or taste like it was intended by the author of the recipe. That is why He is saying: we cannot take suffering out of the life of the Christian. We will never be what He intended us to be. We can live in the city of heaven forever but we will not live there as a king. The Father is giving us the key ingredient that He needs in our lives in order to produce someone just like the Son.

Cup of Suffering

Christ Our Lord drank from a cup called the cup of suffering, and He asked His disciples if they were able to drink of it. Within that cup, when He took up the Cross, and we asked Him to be our Savior, each one of us was handed a cup. We must drink everything that has been allotted to us. It was not ever meant to be optional, for He bought us with His Blood; therefore, He owns us, where we relinquished all of our rights to Him. We must walk through every narrow place, every dark place that has been predestined for us. If we do not, we will

119

not finish our race. We may make it to heaven but finishing our race is overcoming and experiencing everything that He spoke to the churches in the book of Revelation.

The Bible encourages us that as tribulation works patience into our lives, patience brings about experience, and that experience is what brings us hope. We inherit a supernatural hope, because this is our umpteenth tribulation and we know God will come through. Because years passed, we know that He came through over and over again, every time! And that hope causes us not to be ashamed for we know He will do it again.

The love of God is now being shed abroad in our heart because it made our endurance possible, because we obeyed because of our love for Him. We will either love ourselves or Him. And if we refuse to go through sufferings, it is because we love ourselves more than Him. That is what this is about. Suffering will turn the tide of self-centeredness and cause us to love Him more than our own lives.

Rejoice and Be Glad

Rejoice and be exceedingly glad. Barak in Hebrew means to act clamorously foolish. The Lord knows some people do not act foolish until they get drunk. He said be not drunk with wine, but be filled with the Spirit. You drink by praising God, and keep praising God until we start acting foolish. When we start acting foolish, that is exceedingly glad it will cause a title wave of praise to come forth. So, if that means shouting, we have to shout louder than the devil. The devil goes by what he sees us doing on the outside. He does not know what is going on inside of us spiritually. If we keep that rainbow of praise around us that comes forth from the Fruit of the Spirit that is within us, it will thwart his counsel.

Israel put the singers out front and their worship sent up shockwaves until those fools that were against them turned around and started killing each other. Now, if they can do that under an Old Covenant then what can we do under a renewed one with better promises? We cannot be moved by how we feel, or by what we see. We have to be moved by what we believe. When it is all said and done, we are going to respond according to what we believe. Like Smith Wigglesworth said, *"If the Holy Ghost does not move, I will move the Holy Ghost."* You might say, I am not feeling anything. Well, shout and scream until you do feel the help of the Holy Spirit coming.

If We Suffer, We Shall Reign with Him

What is it about persecution and suffering that is good for us?

2 Timothy 2:12
If we suffer, we shall also reign with him: if we deny him, he also will deny us

Notice Timothy says in this verse, *"If we..."* God's Word often has conditions that we must meet in order to qualify for the blessing He wants to give us. Reigning with Him is not automatic, it requires our suffering. At the same time, as we suffer for His sake, He will give us the satisfaction of kicking some devil butt on this side of the grave. When we get to heaven there will be no more devil butt to kick; We are just reigning. But on this earth, we have a chance to reign and do devil butt kicking too and laugh at the devil in the process. So, there is a connection between suffering and qualifying us to reign with the Lord in the Millennial Reign, and into the Eternal Kingdom Age.

Romans 8:17
And if children then heirs. Heirs of God joint heirs with Christ.

When you talk about heirs, we need to think about glory and light. Notice, there is that word "if" again, because He knows human nature and how most love only their own life. It is not possible to suffer with Him, if we are not willing to die to self – our will. We cannot suffer without giving up our lives. That is not saying we do not have plans. We plan this, we plan that but when our plans start running contrary to God's plans, we need to give up our plans. When God says turn left, we need to turn left, even though our plans may say turn right. Remember, suffering is already divinely designed as a part of our lives; it has been predetermined. It is in our cup of suffering. Its goal is to crush us to mold and conform us into His likeness, into His divine character.

The problem with most Christians is that they want the glory before the suffering. Those are the folks that want to be seen and heard. If we were to stand in the throne room and the Father was sitting on the throne, we would not be able to see His face for the brightness and radiance of His light. But we would be able to recognize parts of His body. He shines brighter in the face. That is why the Bible says the glory that shines in the face of Christ. But guess what? His body does not shine as bright as the glory in His face. Yet, His body is still connected to His head. In the same way, we are His Body and as a joint heir we will be connected to Him. We do not shine as bright as Him, but we are still connected to Him. And, we are now compatible with Him because we suffered with Him.

On earth, we see His divine order when a man and woman come together in marriage. The husband is not better than his wife, but they are to complement one another. And, while doing so, there is a compatibility thing that is taking place between them. Under the New Covenant, the relationship between the man and the woman is not that the husband rules over the wife without her having any input. She does not call her husband, Lord. That is the Old Covenant relationship. In the New Covenant both are side by side. He is King and she is Queen and Christ our Lord is the head over them both, and the husband and wife rule together. Yes, there is the domestic side of life, where he can do some things better and she can do something better. Who said the man had to control the checkbook? It is whoever that does not have the spending finger. If the man has the spending finger, then the wife has to hold the checkbook. Its strengths and weaknesses. They come together, compatibility. But both are ruling together. This is New Covenant marriage. The Church needs to come out from under the Old Covenant. So, the head has His part and the Body has its part. The toe does not think because it does not have a brain in it. Wisdom is coming from the head, where the rest of the body can do nothing without the head.

Mortality Will Put on Immortality

Romans 8:18

For I reckon that the sufferings of this present time are not worthy to be compared with the glory which shall be revealed in us.

Now, we really need to get a hold of this scripture because every time we decide not to suffer, we are saying that suffering can be compared to the glory. We are putting the suffering above the glory. But Paul is telling us that the sufferings we go through cannot be compared to the glory which will be revealed inside of us. What does revealed mean? When mortality shall put on immortality. When what is inside of us swallows up the outside. And the degree of light that has grown in us, becomes the platform for our willingness to suffer for him.

We may not see it now, but Christ our Lord gave us a demonstration on the top of Mount Transfiguration. What was on the inside of Him came to the outside and He shined like the sun. His clothes glistened. That is what we have to look forward to, brothers and sisters. One day that is going to happen but it is solely based upon us allowing ourselves to suffer.

So, these scriptures show that persecution and suffering, if responded to rightly, has a way of preparing us for the great things of God. That we may do greater works on this earth than He did. This is what the Church has missed as a whole. Especially, in this generation, because everything now is prosperity and self-centeredness. God does not want us to be unhappy, they say, He wants us to be joyous! But true joy can only come forth when sufferings have done their work within our soul and sorrow and grief is manifested. No amount of material wealth, possessions or people can bring us true joy. Happiness is based on circumstances that can change overnight. But joy is based upon truth. Joy is based upon what we know is at the end of our sufferings. So, it is not so much the suffering in itself but our response to it that is important.

How are you Responding?

James 1:2
My brethren, count it all joy when ye fall into divers temptations;

How are you responding to what you are going through? Diver tests are persecutions against our soul, spirit or body. It has been said that suffering and trouble will either make you bitter or better. Where are you now? Are you being made better or bitter? If you are being made bitter, you must decide to be made better and the only way to do that is to understand what I am saying to you now. That is why James said after the word temptations; *"Knowing this, that the trying of your faith worketh patience."* It is what you know that happens during this process that will determine your response.

Many have not known and they have been made bitter by their Christian life, instead of better. If that is the case, I can guarantee that you are not being made perfect in love either, because you must love the ones that persecute you. How much you are willing to drink of your cup of suffering will determine your level of growth in love. So do not lose your first love! Remember, the first time He went inside of you and you were so in love. Do not let the world and sufferings in your life separate you from that love. Instead, grow in it. It is just the opposite of what the world says we are to do.

Brothers and Sisters, all of our cups are different because we all are different. Remember, everything that God put inside of us as a human was lost when sin swallowed it up and redefined us. But He brought it back when He came into us as a Seed. Everything that we need is in Christ. But it has to grow. We have two seeds within us. Just like there were two trees in the Garden. The Tree of Life and The Tree of the Knowledge of good and Evil. Those two trees are growing together on the inside of us. The enemy planted his tree and the Lord planted His, which is Christ our Lord Himself. The Lord is letting them both grow together, this is the cup of suffering which is taking up your cross.

The Throne of our Soul

Every single ground He gains in our lives – in our souls, He comes and sits on the throne of our soul in that area that we have surrendered to Him, until He sits on every throne in our soul. He comes to bring a total restoration, as we mature into sons of God. That is what we are fighting for – the restoration of our soul. Our spirit has already been saved, and it grows spiritually as our soul is restored.

So these foundational, spiritual principles that are in the Beatitudes, we have to keep meditating on and keep telling ourselves this is what we must do. We must remind ourselves, that we are blessed and not cursed, when these divers' tests come into our lives. At the same time, not forgetting there are certain things that we must do in order for God to do His part. Every place in the Beatitudes we must go through; we must go through the negative to get to the positive. *"Blessed are they which are persecuted for righteousness' sake: for theirs is the kingdom of heaven."*

If we do not go through the sufferings, our position, statue and rank in the Kingdom is not secure.

* * *

Chapter 9: Blessed are the Reviled

Let us summarize a little before moving into Matthew 5:11.

Blessed are the meek

That is an identity in Christ. If we maintain and pursue that meekness, what is the end result? *"For they shall inherit the earth."* God presents us with a characteristic and says, *"This is on the other side, if we pursue meekness."* For they shall inherit the earth means: the earth will not stop producing for us. It will play a part in protecting us; therefore, the meek shall inherit the earth. Paul talks about it in Romans chapter 7 how the earth is moaning for the manifestation of the sons of God. The earth is waiting for us to rise and take our place to bring relief to them from the agony of sin. Believe it or not this is actually preaching the gospel to God's creation, when we command it to respond to us free of the enemy's curse. This is what Matthew is saying in a totally different way. It is those who are meek that the earth will bow down and surrender to.

Blessed are those who hunger and thirst after righteousness

What is the end result? We will be filled, and ultimately, filled with His love. In the same way when we sit down to eat a meal. We have our cornbread, fried chicken, collard greens, sweet potatoes, all different types of food. All of it together fills us up. As we are filled with the Fruit of the Spirit, which is the character of our Father, we begin to feast upon the Lord, His word, His presence. In the same way, as we feed on His righteousness, on His goodness and meekness, we will be filled with those attributes of His divine nature. Ultimately, all that together fills us with His love.

Blessed are they who are merciful for they will be shown mercy

Every opportunity we get, we need to show mercy because we are going to need some down the road. It is one of those things where we might not have enough. Have you ever gone through a grocery store line where you thought you had enough coins to pay for your goods, but found out that you did not? But then someone hands you the coins that you need. That is the way mercy works. When we do not have enough to get us to where we need to be. Then God either brings someone else to help or the Holy Spirit will make up our deficit enabling us to keep moving forward.

129

Blessed are the pure in heart

Speaks to a process that should be happening in every believer's life. It is a purification of whatever God is after in our lives to make our character compatible with His. It may feel like the Holy Spirit is drilling in our flesh. This is a part of the process; the agony of the Holy Spirit going after the weaknesses in our lives. As He does, all the emotions and thoughts of past things that we had long forgotten about will surface. For when the Holy Spirit hits it with his spiritual drill, it unleashes thoughts and memories that have not been dealt with and healed. He is digging deep, where He is after the removal of the root. That ultimately leads to purity of heart. The purer we become, the more He pulls back the veil and the darkness in that area of our lives, and the clearer we can literally see the Lord.

Blessed are the Peacemakers

These are people who do not take anything personally. That is a mature person. Remember the parable that Christ our Lord spoke to Israel? He said I sent you this prophet, I sent you that prophet. They came with the Word of the Lord and the message of peace, and you killed each one. The King then said, I will send my son; they will hear him, but they killed him. What did the angels sing? Peace on earth because the Prince of Peace came, who is the Peacemaker. Although He was God when He came into the earth realm, by spiritual definition He was not. There was a price that Christ Our Lord had to pay by learning obedience. Then God spoke out of heaven and said, "This is My beloved Son." The Peacemaker, Who surrendered Himself, has matured bringing the Word of the Lord. Christ our Lord humbled Himself, being willing to be a target. In the court system they call that person a mediator. A mediator must be willing to take all the crap and cussing from the other person, because they are the peacemaker. The one who is trying to make peace. This is what the Lord offers us as an aspect of His character, but it will cost us everything.

Blessed are those who are persecuted for righteousness' sake, for theirs is the Kingdom of heaven

These are those who are willing, again, to put themselves in harm's way so that the Kingdom of God can be advanced. When they do, the Kingdom of God is growing on the inside of them. Christ our Lord said, *"The Kingdom of God does not come with observation."* It is something that is happening on the inside of people. But for that to happen, we are going to be persecuted.

Haters of Those Who do Good

Timothy said in the last days there will be haters of those who do good. We will be hated simply because we decide to be nice – to be kind, and by turning the other cheek. Walking in love will cause us to be hated. We see that polarization is happening in our nation right now, especially in politics. I thought it would show up in religious circles first. It is about to happen in the Church today, as it did in Christ Our Lord's' day.

Christ our Lord came with truth and people got angry. They got so angry and hateful that they killed Him. They killed every one of the disciples, except John. And that same polarization and great divide is happening today. This is the Lord's doing. What is happening in our nation today, He is using it to force people to choose whom they want to serve. The result is showing what is really in people's hearts, with all their deceit and deception. Their hatred is so great that they want to shut down our free speech. They do not want to hear what others have to say, that opposes their wicked views.

I want to emphasize, all the character assassination that we are seeing in politics today is coming to the Church. The scripture calls it leprosy of the tongue. We are going to have to be overflowing with the characteristics that are found in the Beatitudes to maintain our poise, and to be able to walk in love towards those that hate us. We have to remember that we are being attacked because of our position in Christ, it is for righteousness' sake. That positioning enables us to possess the Kingdom. We are not talking about going into heaven and possessing the Kingdom. We are talking about the Kingdom being fortified inside of us now, which brings heaven to earth.

Matthew 5:11

Blessed are ye, when men shall revile you, and persecute you, and shall say all manner of evil against you falsely, for my sake.

We cannot counter punch as a Christian; we are not to fight by carnal means. If we are going to punch someone let it be directed at the devil. Our war is not against flesh and blood. This war is coming to the Church and we must have enough inside of us not to retaliate. We have to learn to not take things personally, because it is for righteousness' sake. This must be firmly in our foundation. We must take the position of

Matthew 5:12 and rejoice and be exceedingly glad when we are persecuted and reviled, even when others get physical with us. We cannot do that in our own strength. It is easier said than done, but if we have allowed the Holy Spirit to keep us on the path, with each turn, confrontation and situation, He has built something in us and taken something out of us, enabling us to overcome. The result is when we find ourselves in these situations, we will be able to rejoice. It is a part of our Christian walk to be persecuted, to be tested and tried. So, rejoice! Be exceedingly glad, for we will need that exceedingly, exhilarating joy to carry us through the battles.

Persecution and Suffering Prepare Us

2 Timothy 2:12
If we suffer, we shall also reign with him: if we deny him, he also will deny us:

Romans 8:17
And if children, then heirs; heirs of God, and joint-heirs with Christ; if so be that we suffer with him, that we may be also glorified together.

These verses show that if persecution and suffering are responded to rightly, they have a way of preparing us for great things in God. It is not so much the suffering, but how we respond to it. This is what the Beatitudes is about; how we are responding to the things that come against us. It has been said suffering and trouble will make you better or bitter. Ultimately, it is up to us to choose how we want to respond. In the midst of suffering, God deals not just with what we are doing, but

133

more so why we are doing it.

Let us look at the story of Job, again. A lot of things have been misconstrued concerning Job. Early on in my walk, I heard how others used Job to teach Christians how to walk by faith. They twisted Job's circumstances to fit the narrative of the faith message. I heard things like: if you are not healed instantly, then you do not have enough faith. Well, I saw early on that was a half-truth. For instance, God does not bring sickness and disease, but He sure will take advantage of it. To the Lord, pain is pain and suffering is suffering. If we allow Him, He will work it for our good. We can bring pain and suffering into our lives because of our hard headedness, stupidity or ignorance. Peter said if that is the case, then in a nutshell, this is my paraphrase, we just need to grin and bear it. We have to go through it, so it can be turned for our good, if we do not abandon it. Even when we allowed it into our own lives.

But then there are situations such as Job, even though we are not perfect, where many things in our lives are not the results of anything bad that we did. Often, it is the results of what someone else did. We may have made decisions afterwards that were not helpful, but those decisions were in direct correlation to what had been done to us. So, God takes this all into consideration and in so doing, He has to allow certain things in our lives to uproot things out of our lives that are killing us. Do you understand what I am saying? Even when He allows it, sometimes we make bad decisions concerning the remedy, because we resist it. Because it appears like it is bringing more pain instead of removing our pain.

So was the case with Job, and the Bible brings into focus a man who God wanted to bless. In my early walk with the Lord that was not what I had heard. However, God could only bring Job to a larger place through suffering, and that is the case with all of us. It was the case with the Lord. He learned obedience through the things He suffered. As Christ suffered in the flesh, so too should we arm ourselves to do likewise. He is talking about knowledge now, but knowledge with the same mind as Christ. And, not just knowledge, but we need to arm ourselves with the same tools that will enable us to go through our suffering, just as He went through His. What am I saying? It is the activities that are taking place in our lives, during suffering, that prepares and arms us to win the next test that we inter into. This is why so many Christians are weak and fall apart at every turn when faced with afflictions. We are called overcomers because we must overcome something. We are not called survivors, but overcomers!

God Uses Suffering to Bless and Not Curse Us

Many Christians are surviving, yet they think they are over-coming. And because they are not overcoming, they are not equipped with what they need to overcome next time. Remember, it is like a piece in a puzzle. Ultimately, when all the pieces are together, the Lord can extract the root. This is what played out in Job's life. The story of Job was put in the Bible as an example of how God uses suffering to bless us, not curse us. God was not mad at Job, He wanted to bless him and that is the narrative that we have to understand. Through this suffering, God was able to bring Job into a place where he was able to qualify him so that He could bless him even more.

Qualifying is a particularly important word in our walk with the Lord. Job qualified for advancement in the Kingdom of

God because of how he chose to overcome his sufferings. Like the experience of Isaiah, who found himself in the manifest presence of God, and as a result when his eyes were opened, he saw his sinful nature. A lot of people do not see their sinful nature because there is not a level of purity that has happened to them. That is why, if we are going to go deeper in the Lord, we must go deeper in repentance, because when He peels us like an onion, we are going to see something about ourselves that we did not presently see. The only thing God mentioned in the beginning concerning Job's life is the fear that Job had. If Job had great fear, there was something else in his life that should not have been there that allowed him to have that fear.

Job 3:25-26

For the thing which I greatly feared has come upon me, and that which I was afraid of is come unto me. I was not in safety, neither had rest, neither was I quiet; yet trouble came.

But if we read Job chapter one, we find that he was in safety. But Job could not read chapter one because it was not written, yet. So, we know that he was in safety, because the Bible says the sons of God presented themselves before the throne of God. And God said, *"What are you doing?"* Their response was: we are just cruising throughout the earth, looking for people's lives we can ruin.

Fear Paralyzes

God had not turned against Job, instead, He was ready to bless him even more. But He could not with fear dominating his life. God knew that the best way to get fear out of his life was to take Job through what he went through. Why did Job not see the obvious? There is something about fear that will paralyze a person. It opens the door to the realm of the spirit. I was so bombarded by a spirit of fear in my life that the spirits almost started to manifest. I never saw their faces; I saw their hands around my neck at night. They would pull me out of a sound sleep with their hands around my neck. These demons were able to do so, because fear eventually opens the door to the realm of the spirit. The only way you can close that door is by faith. Nobody had to cast a demon of fear out of me. I closed it by faith when I realized my authority in the name of Christ Our Lord. At the time, I had sufficient faith but I was not releasing it with words of faith. When the spirit of fear comes into your sphere of influence, it brings the feeling of fear; the temptation to be afraid.

When the enemy plans an attack against us, fear, nine times out of ten is amongst the demons that are in that group sent to attack us, though there are other spirits, as well. They come because there are weaknesses in our lives, and those spirits possess power over those weaknesses. Fear will come into our mind and bring awareness of the weaknesses. They can always tell when and where a person is ready to be attacked. That fear tries to cripple you by bringing other little imps into the realm of the spirit to attack the area where you are afraid so that you cannot overcome it. This weakness, insecurity – or whatever the case may be, are all spirits that run together. They have an assignment from the devil. The Bible calls them the works of the flesh, and every work of the flesh has a spirit – or demon, that specializes in that very thing. I mention this because many Christians are aware of the persecution that comes against them on the outside, but not what the enemy is using within them.

Fear is a Power

Let me give an example. Say you are single and you know that you cannot fornicate anymore. So here comes fear – fear that you will not be able to stay pure and chaste, and with fear comes lust and the devil's other cronies. Lust will not come out first, it will be fear. Fear will harness the strength of the other spirits; the power that they possess. The Bible calls them powers. It is because they possess a particular power. In this case, it would be lust. You must pray through this, because you do not have what it takes to overcome that weakness without God's grace, or you would have already.

Another example is with alcohol. You have been sober for a while. Then out of the blue your taste buds want alcohol. It is those demons pressuring you. The devil waits until you are depressed, down and out. When you are feeling like you do not have a friend in the world. Then here comes fear targeting a particular weakness, although it is alcohol that has the power and wants access. Yet, it is fear that kicks down the door. That is not the time to drive by the bar or search for your old drinking buddies. That is the time that you need to get alone with the Lord.

Or, here is another tactic the devil uses: when we lose one battle, we just throw away the war. Other words, you say to yourself, I might as well go for it and drink the whole bottle! That is the mentality the devil gives us. This is the situation with Job. But when you know God's ways, you know eventually the Father is going to have to deal with all weakness in your life. Thank God, He does not do it all at once! Instead, one by one, He will walk you through the valley of the shadow of death and allow your weakness to persecute you from within through suffering.

Such as Job, God would not allow these situations in our lives, if He were not ready to promote us and bring the victory. During these times, the number one weapon in our arsenal must be prayer. James 5:13 said, *"Is any among you afflicted? Let him pray."* Get filled up while listening to the Holy spirit and get the strategy of heaven for how to overcome.

There will be times when God will allow the devil to access our weaknesses. But God will set the parameters, where the devil will only be able to touch the weaknesses that the Father allows. *"There is no temptation taken you."* We will not be tempted above that which we are able. So understand brothers and sisters, it is not going to go away. Our purpose in praying, in the midst of the test, is so that we can be empowered and get the wisdom and counsel of God to overcome.

Spirit of Persecution

2 Corinthians 12:7-11

And lest I should be exalted above measure through the abundance of the revelations, there was given to me a thorn in the flesh, the messenger of Satan to buffet me, lest I should be exalted above measure.**8** For this thing I besought the Lord thrice, that it might depart from me.**9** And he said unto me, My grace is sufficient for thee: for my strength is made perfect in weakness. Most gladly therefore will I rather glory in my infirmities, that the power of Christ may rest upon me.**10** Therefore I take pleasure in infirmities, in reproaches, in necessities, in persecutions, in distresses for Christ's sake: for when I am weak, then am I strong.

There are deep mysteries in these verses but we will address just one. Notice Paul said there was given to me a thorn because of the abundance of revelation. This is not just something that happened to Paul because he was an apostle. It happens to all of us because it is a spiritual law. Remember the parable of the sower and how the enemy came immediately afterwards because of the Word sown. Paul wrote over two-thirds of the New Testament. The Word that was sown into him by the Holy Spirit is what brought a spirit of persecution into his life. It exposed weaknesses in his life within and without. He had to take God's grace, which comes to us through knowledge according to Peter, and overcome it. This is why Paul says, *"I glory in it."* He found a mystery in suffering for the cause of the Cross. It was learning to overcome in this world, especially the things inside of us that are not like the Lord.

Now you can see what I mean when people revile against you or persecute you. Though it is an act coming at you from without, what is going on inside of you will determine your response. Therefore, we need to spend more time on what is happening within us and how it is working against us, than the many things that can come against us. Example; we see how Christ our Lord responded to the devil while in the wilderness. Satan was trying to access something within the Lord but there was nothing there to access.

Job 42:5
I have heard of thee by the hearing of the ear:

That is the problem with most Christians. They have heard of God in certain areas, but they have not experienced Him. There is a reason the Bible calls it the fellowship of His suffering, because in the midst of suffering is when we get to know the character of Christ Our Lord. Job goes on to say, *"Now my eyes seeth thee."* Because during suffering, a veil of darkness is removed and our ability to see the Lord increases. This is the process and there is no way around it, if we want to grow up and become a son of God. We can keep getting sovereign blessings, but guess what? Sovereign acts of God will not cause us to grow up. They simply deliver us. Equally, ministers of the gospel who are anointed with giftings and callings, those things do not cause them to grow up. It is when they experience their own difficulties and strongholds and suffer through them, His way. That is what will cause them to grow up and be delivered.

Job 42:6
Wherefore I abhor myself, and repent in dust and ashes.

In verse 6, Job tells us that seeing God allows us to see ourselves more. And when we do, we repent in dust and ashes. Once we go through a trial and we have been delivered, then the presence of God comes upon us in a glorious way bringing times of refreshing. God determines the length of time between all those things. When we enter into a higher level in God, it requires deeper repentance. What Christ our Lord secured for us on the Cross comes to us through repentance. Then God in turn gives us the tools to help Him to restore our soul. He does it line upon line, precept upon precept. It is not something that happens automatically. We understand that more now because of what we talked about, the four different ways that God helps to restore the soul, and it is our responsibility to persevere.

Principle of Deliverance

Look at what Job 42:10 says:

> **Job 42:10**
> And the Lord turned the captivity of Job when he prayed for his friends.

The Lord gave Job twice as much as he had before. That is the principle of deliverance. In New Covenant, it is more than twice, it is a seven-fold restitution. Hallelujah! We see in this verse that Job's attitude towards his friends who had tormented him has changed. Many times, God brings people into our lives to help us change. In this particular case, only one of Job's counselors was right; the other three were off all the time. They were jealous of Job from the beginning: jealous of his spirituality, jealous of his wealth and material gain.

The moment that Job fell, they were saying, Job, you deserved it. It is because of this and that. The Bible says they all lied. We can see job has another thing to deal with now – his friends turning against him. So, that gives us a glimpse that Job had a problem in the area of his character, as well. In his love walk, as well. This is why God targeted him, as some people who do us no good, we will only see occasionally. Think about it, what if they came to your house and camped out in your front yard? That is what they did to Job, they came and camped out with him. Think about that narrative, we only have to deal with our accusers occasionally. Job had a problem to overcome; was he going to let these people destroy him or walk in forgiveness.

It is bad enough that he stank, with pus all over him. Scraping his skin with a knife. Then he has all his friends telling him that he deserved it! If he had the gift of tongues, he would have had to do a lot of praying in tongues. Can we see how the enemy will try to divert our progression to get our eyes off God's purpose and plans for our lives? To draw us into an area of the works of the flesh: resentment and strife. When we are going through a test, we have to watch these areas of our lives because if we walk in them, we will prolong our test. And so, was the case with Job his attitude towards his friends changed and he prayed for them. When he prayed for them, he entered into a new place.

Look at what Job 42:12 says:

Job 42:12-13
So the Lord blessed the latter end of Job more than his beginning: for he had fourteen thousand sheep, and six thousand camels, and a thousand yoke of oxen, and a thousand she asses. **13** He had also seven sons and three daughters.

Now remember, Job has a new family as all his children and

servants died. The Bible never says if he got a new woman, but he must have. Seven sons, three daughters. He called the first son Jemima and the name of the second Kezia, and the third Kerenhappuch. And in all the land there were no women found fairer than the daughters of Job. So, that must have been important. Sometimes the anointing of God just beautifies everything. In other words, he had no ugly kids. *"And their father gave them inheritance among their brethren."*

Now this is the pattern of the New Covenant believers. That we should have enough to give to our children's' children. That is what the Bible says. I do not know many Christians like that today. But, if that was not enough, Job lived another 140 years and saw his sons, and his sons' sons, even four generations. *"So, Job died old and full of days."* Brother and Sister, if they can get that under the Old Covenant, we should be far surpassing that under the New Covenant. I guarantee you, at 140 years, Job was not being pushed around in a wheelchair! Full of days implies a life of healing and health.

Greater Levels in God

This story is placed by God in the Bible to show us how we are to obtain greater levels in God. This is the point I want to make; there can be no resurrection life without first a death taking place. There are areas in our lives where the power of the Cross is made available to us through repentance. Suffering has a way of transforming our view of life. We see things differently when we suffer. It brings mercy into our lives and long suffering for someone else. Do you know why you are so impatient? It is because you do not suffer. Blessed are the merciful, for they shall obtain mercy. Well, we do not become merciful at a snap of a finger. We become merciful by suffering. It has a way of ordering the right priorities in our lives. We do not struggle with right priorities anymore after going through deeper levels of suffering. It brings forth a certain amount of revelation making it natural to do. Just as natural as a fish swimming through water. Suffering cuts away at the materialism in our lives. Those things that are not important to us. If we get it fine, if we do not that is just fine, too. It does not control our lives and our lives do not exist in what we possess. If God tells us to give it away, we have no problem doing it. Suffering has a way of severing worthless things and junk from our lives. It cuts away clutter and wrong priorities in our lives. And, it is all preparatory for our advancement in the Kingdom.

Psalms 119:67
Before I was afflicted, I went astray but now have I kept thy word.

That is a principle we need to embrace. It does not simply mean walking away from God, leaving God and totally backsliding. It can mean that, but even more so what are we doing when God is trying to bring our lives back under His control? So, He allows persecution to come when He is after certain things in our lives. Do you go astray? Do you run from suffering like Job did in the beginning, saying, *"Lord, take me. Naked I came, Naked I go."* Do you want the Lord to kill you, like Elijah did? Well, if he really wanted to die Jezebel would have been more than happy to accommodate him. The Lord said to Elijah *"What are you doing here?"* Kill me Lord, kill me, was his response! Jezebel told him she was going to take his head off just like he took all

145

those prophets heads off, so no he did not really want to die. God sees through all of our pity parties, antics and self-focused tears. Are we not glad that a lot of times He does not pay any attention to it? Just like we do not pay attention to our little kids when they say, I hate you. Are we not glad that God does not pay any attention when we start talking crazy, when we are hurting and consumed in our raw emotions?

He is a good Father. So, we need to stop running away from the tests He has allowed in our lives. When we stop running, then we will finally get it like the psalmist said, "But now I keep Your word." Pain tempers the soul making it pliable and receptive to greater levels in God. I learned this year ago and I did what was necessary. When people did not treat me right, I turned the other cheek. When people looked at me, thinking I was going to hold something against them. I did not even think about it. I refused to see them in that light, because it was not worth it.

If we do, it will keep us from growing spiritually. But some might say, *"It is not God's will for me to be in pain, I love the Lord! Christ Our Lord bore our pain so we could be free."* But let me ask the question, when we were saved, were we totally free? There are none of us that are totally free, yet. That is the point of this book. We are free in one sense, where all the darkness and demons were driven out of our spirit man. But many of them just went into our soul and set up camp there, and are hiding out. God has to keep sweeping our soul to cleanse it. And in this case, He gives us the broom. If we do not want it swept out, it will not get swept out. Sometimes pain is the only way God can condition us to be able to receive greater blessings that will move us into greater levels in God.

God Does Not Afflict Us

I want to emphasize this: God does not afflict us. James told us God cannot be tempted with evil nor does He tempt any man. But when God stops protecting the lust of our flesh, that lust now starts tempting our soul. God protects a lot of areas in our lives, just like a parent protects their child. God does that in different seasons of our lives, but when He is ready to promote and bless us, He has to stop protecting us. He will drop His hedge of protection in that area of our lives for a season. Just like a big brother protects his little sister until she can protect and fight for herself. So God does not afflict us but when necessary, He allows the enemy to afflict us in order to bring us to a place where we can hear what God is saying to us and what He wants of us. This was the case with Job.

Job 33:14-15

For God speaketh once, yea twice, yet man perceived it not. In a dream, in a vision of the night, when deep sleep falleth upon men, in slumberings upon the bed;

God has not stopped speaking to us in this way. God has encapsulated new ways because of the New Covenant. God speaks to us through His Word, but Job did not have a Bible. But we do have the Bible so God speaks to us through His Word. He will also speak to us through the Gifts of the Spirit. God can speak to us by appearing to us. But He still uses dreams, visions, visions of the night. It is a little difficult to distinguish between a dream and a vision of the night. If you went to sleep and you thought it was a dream and you made this statement: it was so real. It was like I was there. That was more than a dream. That was a vision in the night. As pertaining to visions, sometimes, you are looking at it, but in others, you participate in it, where God takes your soul and pulls you inside of it.

Job goes on to say, in verse 16, *"Then He openeth the ears of men, and sealeth their instructions."* This is how God does things. He can bypass our finite mind and puts things inside of us that we need to fulfill our purposes. Many times, you wake up and say, "I had the strangest dream." You are trying to understand the dream. But the interpretation is in your spirit. You do not necessarily have to interpret it with your mind, God has sealed instructions on the inside of you. If you are sensitive, if you spend time with the Lord like you are supposed to, waiting on and worshipping Him, then you will automatically start walking out those instructions.

He goes on to say, verse 17-19, *"That He may withdraw man from his purpose, and hide pride from man. He keepeth his soul back from the pit, and his life from perishing by the sword. He is chastened also with pain upon his bed, and the multitude of his bones with strong pain."* Now, for those who are stubborn, then God has to incorporate a little pain. So do not be stubborn like Job.

Verse 20 says, *"So that his life abhorreth bread, and his soul dainty meat."* In other words, God is trying to stop us from feeding on things that are destroying us and our relationship with Him, wanting us to turn inward towards Him. Understand this and settle this once and for all: if you love God, with everything that is in you at this level in your spiritual life and you really want Him, and are doing everything to pursue Him, then know everything that is happening to you is working for your good. We must believe that because the enemy will try to convince us otherwise and cause us to turn away from what God is doing on the inside of us. We will start fighting against Him when we do not understand and when we do not know what to do. Remember, that is the time to rejoice! The Bible says in everything, not for everything, we are to give thanks. We can release faith in praise, when we do, we are saying I do not understand it, but I trust You, Lord.

Verse 21-24 says, *"His flesh is consumed away, that it cannot be seen; and his bones that were not seen stick out."* Job is describing his own experience. He further says, *"Yea, his soul draweth near unto the grave, and his life to the destroyers. If there be a messenger with him, an interpreter one among a thousand, to shew unto man his uprightness: then He is gracious unto him."*

Well, we have an interpreter, the Holy Spirit. Job did not understand the working of the Holy Spirit in his day. They believed everything whether it was good or bad, that God did it. They blamed Him for everything, but we know differently. Verse 25 says, *"His flesh shall be fresher than a child's: He shall return to the days of his youth: He shall pray unto God, and He will be favourable unto him: and he shall see his face with joy: for he will render unto man His righteousness."*

Principles We Can Follow Today

So, can we see it was God's wisdom that took Job's life, and through his life Job wrote principles about a righteous God. Principles that we can follow today. So, when the work of suffering has finished, great healing comes and a new place in God is achieved.

Romans 8:18

For I reckon that the suffering of this present time are not worthy to be compared with the glory which shall be revealed in us."

That is what we must keep telling ourselves, as well, "We look not at the things that are seen but at the things that are not seen." The more we hurt, the more we are in pain, we have to keep telling ourselves: the glory is around the corner. This is transformation. It is much more than the presence of God. This is a manifestation of His glory, where He takes a part of His spirit and puts it inside of us and it becomes a part of us. It is something that we carry with us all the time (Philippians 1:29, Colossians 1:24, James 5:10-11).

So, remember there are many kinds of suffering of which pain is just one. I can talk to Christians, look into their life and see that they are suffering. Sometimes, they do not even realize they are suffering because there are many kinds. Whatever God allows you to go through, He will use it as a stepping stone to glory. If you have not, you need to accept the fact and settle it once and for all that everything that happens in your life is working for your good, because you love Him. I know it can be hard sometimes because we cannot see the future. Even when you realize that you have allowed things into your life that were not the will of God because of pride, bad decisions and immaturity. Well, when you come into the knowledge of something and walking in that truth now, trust God to turn those things around for your good, because He will! Amen!

* * *

Chapter 10: Summary

Matthew 5:1-11 (KJV)

And seeing the multitudes, he went up into a mountain: and when he was set, his disciples came unto him:² And he opened his mouth, and taught them, saying,³ Blessed are the poor in spirit: for theirs is the kingdom of heaven.⁴ Blessed are they that mourn: for they shall be comforted.⁵ Blessed are the meek: for they shall inherit the earth.⁶ Blessed are they which do hunger and thirst after righteousness: for they shall be filled.⁷ Blessed are the merciful: for they shall obtain mercy.⁸ Blessed are the pure in heart: for they shall see God.⁹ Blessed are the peacemakers: for they shall be called the children of God.¹⁰ Blessed are they which are persecuted for righteousness' sake: for theirs is the kingdom of heaven.¹¹ Blessed are ye, when men shall revile you, and persecute you, and shall say all manner of evil against you falsely, for my sake.

We have looked at these series of messages that Christ our Lord preached to inspect our house, known as the Beatitudes. To see clearly what the Lord is saying, and how we are to apply these principles to our lives, and how the Holy Spirit can shine His Light upon us even more.

The Sermon on the Mount is the foundation upon which everything is built in retrospect to the New Testament. The Sermon on the Mount is the principles and teachings from the ten commandments. It is where the disciples got all of their teachings, spiritual foundations, doctrines and principles. It is an exposé of Kingdom requirements. The essentials of a Kingdom lifestyle. In retrospect to enduring or lasting as a believer in this world the bible speaks about two main principles. The parable of the sower or the man that built his house, each speaks to the overcomer's life and you growing up in the kingdom of God. However, in this book we approached it more from the basics of the hindrances you will encounter from your sowing or building or rather how God has chosen to develop you. The end results being a firm foundation and the character of our King.

Beautiful Attitudes

The word Beatitude comes from the Latin word "beatus," which means blessed. In other words, the Lord is saying to you and me if we want to be truly blessed, then these beautiful attitudes need to become a part of who we are in every facet of our lives. Paul said that we are to add to our faith virtue and knowledge. These beautiful attitudes are something that we immediately need to add to the foundation stone of our house, which is Christ our Lord Himself. When we do, they will bring out the character of Christ Our Lord that is in us, so that what is destructive to us is destroyed.

These kingdom laws are what the King requires of those who wish to become joint heirs of this Kingdom. When people are preparing to buy a house, they hire professional inspectors to inspect it to make sure that they are not getting cheated. The Lord has given us these beautiful attitudes to inspect our lives and if these qualities of the Kingdom are not a part of our lives, then we are just loud sounding brass and tinkling symbols who are no threat to the enemy.

Because we are called into His army to fight, we must carry our own weight spiritually. Our two main objectives, as a believer, should be becoming like Him and fulfilling our destiny. Some may say, "Well I just want to be a good mother and raise my kids." But we have to know that we have a purpose beyond that – being a parent is just an extra job that we are to do!

A Purpose Within Us

The Lord put within us a purpose and that is how He determines our value to Him. Stop and think about it from a natural standpoint. In our businesses would we fire our best employees that are making us money? Of course not!

This is what the scripture is talking about when the husbandman comes into his field and he starts inspecting it. Where he sees a tree in the field that has been there a long time and it has not produced any fruit. He tells them to cut it down, but grace speaks out and says Father, "Give me a little more time to dig around it and fertilize it, and see if it will bring forth fruit." You know what that means, right? It is about pouring grace upon our lives enabling us to go through the troubles and tribulations that will bring us to a place of brokenness in our lives. That brokenness causes us to grow and helps us to break out of the traps and snares of stagnation that had prevented us from growing.

So, brother and sister, to the degree and measure that God can bring brokenness in our lives and suffering in our lives is to the degree we will be valuable in the Kingdom. And the purpose for which He created us is being called forth. Unfortunately, because darkness is being reaped at the same pace and intensity that Light is being reaped, the Lord will be forced to bring many of His children home.

We are entering into the age of great deception where believers are one step from perdition, where many will cross a line that they cannot come back from. So the grace, mercy and goodness of God will be to take them home early. This is where we are today, yet the Lord has given us a blueprint to help prepare ourselves so that we can become one with Him, for that is His desire and perfect will for all.

Non-compatibility with Him

But the problem that we have in our relationship with the Lord is our non-compatibility with Him. The only way the Lord can make us compatible is to come to us. But He has refrained from doing that because of a lack of purity in His house. The cry has gone out and if we listen in the Spirit, we can hear it: behold the Bridegroom cometh – He is coming! The Word says He shall come suddenly to His temple. That is us, brothers and sisters!

He is awakening those who have made themselves ready. There has to be a level of purity so that something may not only happen to us, but happens through us. Christ Our Lord came not just to redeem us, but to reveal the Father to us. In John 14, He said My Father will love those who keep His commandments and because they do, He will bring the Father to us. Christ Our Lord is going to introduce us to the Father.

In Christ Our Lord's' earth walk, He demonstrated the Father everywhere He went. It was a demonstration of His pure, unadulterated love that was revealed in the Sermon on the Mount. We must get a fresh look at our Christian values because they are eroding before our very eyes. We can see that in our Nation – a Nation that was founded and built on Judeo-Christian values.

The difficulties in the Church are because of the lack of a foundation that is built on truth. That is why there is so much mixture in the Body of Christ. And it is why the Lord has chosen suffering and persecution as a proving ground for us, not only to prove our love towards Him, but to help us always understand where we stand in Him. The enemy is banking that we will go into the battle that rages all around us unequipped. But as our love for the Lord grows, He in turn takes the love that we have for Him and thrust us into the battle to destroy darkness. I am not a Star Wars fan but it beautifully depicts what will happen to much of the Church in these last days, in how many will be pulled over to the dark side. Much of the Church has not allowed the Lord to help them be placed on the Cross. And because of this fact, many in the Church have a false sense of security.

The Cross – A Death to Self

The Sermon on the Mount brings the Cross into focus. This is what has been lacking in the Church. We want resurrection power, but nobody wants to die. So when the Holy Spirit starts allowing us to feel those things of the past that are stopping our growth – pain, bitterness, jealousy, things that we didn't even know were there or we thought were long gone, we often miss the blessed opportunity to deny ourselves and take up our crosses. And for most of us, it is stuff that we have no idea how it got a hold of us. Do not fool yourself, just because you can quote a few scriptures, it is only through death to self and subsequent resurrection that we become the qualities required to live in a Kingdom realm.

Paul at the height of his ministry, said I am crucified with Christ. He is letting us know how he accomplished what he accomplished. I am crucified, nevertheless, I live, yet it is not I that lives, but Christ Who lives within me. It sounds like an oxymoron, right? But Paul is showing the intertwining, the oneness process that comes through crucifixion. Christ Our Lord is the only One Who has the best personality and is blameless. Christ Our Lord is the only One Who is without fault. Everything about us is flawed. He died to give us Himself. He that knew no sin, became sin for us that we might be made the righteousness of God in Him.

So, Christ Our Lord set the standard when He went to the Cross: if we want Him, we must die. The Christ that is in me as seed has grown up and come to the forefront. Now He possesses me. He is living His life through me. And the life I now live in the flesh, I live by the faith of the Son of God who loves me. If we believe that, then we must believe everything in our lives is working for our good. We have to look at it from the Lord's perspective. This is one reason why the Lord allows the pain and suffering in our lives. So we can get back what the enemy stole seven-fold restitution. Our suffering is redemptive, if we go through it His way, but most Christians do not believe that everything is working for their good. We must believe that, if we are going to become like Him. Because Christ Our Lord is the only One Who can turn our pain into joy and gladness.

Galatians 6:14
But God forbid that I should glory, save in the cross of our Lord Jesus Christ, by whom the world is crucified unto me, and I unto the world.

Paul is saying, I realize what my obedience has brought me. I see what it has done for me and to me, but God forbid that I should glory save in the Cross of our Lord. It is because of the Cross that I am where I am. God forbid that I glory in anything except the Cross of our Lord Jesus Christ by whom is crucified unto me, and I unto the world. Every time we nail ourselves to the Cross, we lose our desire for the world. That is His perfect and eternal intent!

My Yoke is Easy and My Burden is Light

Brothers and Sisters, we need to understand that when we are getting ready to lay a foundation with blocks, the mason man drops a plumb line on the blocks to make sure the foundation is straight. If this is done correctly, then everything he does subsequently becomes easier and easier. That is why Christ Our Lord said My yoke is easy and My burden is light. I can guarantee you, if there is great struggle with no apparent victory in our lives, it is because we are not doing what He says to do. There are many in the Church who do not have a good foundation. This is why they are struggling even to maintain little principles in the Bible that they should have long been past and grounded in.

Matthew 5:5

Blessed are the meek for they shall inherit the earth.

Listen to what the Lord is saying. Blessed are the meek, or the humble, for they shall inherit the earth. He has to be talking primarily about the Millennial Reign. And not just the Millennial Reign, but the new earth and the new heaven. Most of the Church, bless their hearts, believe God is going to empty out heaven during the Millennial Reign and bring them all back to the earth. NO, He isn't! The only ones coming back are those who have graduated – those who have passed their tests. Let me use terminology that the Bible uses; those who overcame. That is who will be coming back with Him, and the first step, the first qualification – the first brick, or first aspect of one's character that must be prevalent in one's life is meekness.

The Greek word for meek is *"praus"* (prah-oos), which means "humble." Humility is an absolute essential quality, if we are to walk with the Lord and inherit the earth.

God Resists the Proud

So we may ask ourselves, are we a humble person? Do we feel like God is resisting us? If we do, it is because we are not humble, for God resists the proud. When we are in the midst of suffering and God is in the midst of breaking our character, He does this by dropping the hedge of protection in our lives. Why does He do this? To expose those things in our lives that are harming us, and our number one enemy will be our pride. We do not need that in our lives because we need help from heaven, and the last person that we need resisting us, is God. God resists the proud but gives grace to the humble.

This is why the Lord says that it is the meek, who shall inherit the earth. It is a part of our responsibility to get it back, because God gave it to us. It is a part of our inheritance. For to inherit the earth is to advance the Kingdom – it is to win, but we have to deal with our own lives in order to do so.

Matthew 5:6
Blessed are they which do hunger and thirst after righteousness, for they shall be filled.

Building block number two: blessed are those who hunger and thirst after righteousness for they will be filled. This is a missing ingredient in the Church because if we are hungering and thirsting for righteousness, there would be evidence of it in our lives. There would be sacrifices made in our lives on every level – spiritually, emotionally, physically and financially, to get God. A question we must ask ourselves: what kind of sacrifices are we making in order to get a hold of Him? We cannot afford to do business as usual anymore. We cannot do Christian living as usual. If we want to go further into His plans for us, then things must change. It is time to be desperate. We have to live every day like we are going to live to be 100 years old, but at the same time like we are going to die tomorrow. In that desperation, we have to finish our race, before we die.

With that desperation we cannot let up, we cannot make excuses. That has to be our mentality now. That is what He is saying. It is those who hunger and thirst after righteousness who shall be filled. The more that we are filled by the Holy Spirit, the more we want to eat and drink of Him. The more we will be compelled to make sacrifices to do what is necessary to become like Him in our words, thoughts and deeds. I am not talking about religious stuff.

So, how do we know if we are being filled with the right thing? If we look into our life right now and we are not crying out on the inside of our soul, for the Lord constantly, then we are not hungering and thirsting after righteousness. It should be evident of what is driving us, what is compelling us, what is on our mind, and what we are moving towards.

Matthew 5:7

Blessed are the merciful, for they shall obtain mercy.

Building block number three: blessed are the merciful for they will be shown mercy. You know it is impossible to be merciful without being meek. To be merciful just simply means: be nice to people. Blessed are the merciful for they shall obtain mercy. So, if we are showing mercy to others, then when we need it, God will be merciful towards us. If we are not merciful, then we will not qualify to receive it.

Matthew 5:8

Blessed are the pure in heart, for they shall see God.

Listen to what Christ Our Lord is saying in verse eight – He is building a foundation. He is linking a chain together that becomes stronger and stronger with each link. "Blessed are the **pure** in heart, for **they** shall see God." The Word of God has multiple layers and several depths of revelation in it. When we peel back one layer of revelation, we will become pure, we will do what it takes to be purified. We allow the Holy Spirit to break us. We are nailing ourselves to the Cross. This will happen from glory to glory. We will see God and His revelation in His Word, before we ultimately lay our spiritual eyes upon Him.

Again, this is another reason He is coming to us. The veil will be pulled back, the scales will fall from our eyes and we enter in through the door in our spirit. "Blessed are the pure in heart for they shall see God." There are a lot of saints in heaven who will never see God in His full glory, for He dwells in unapproachable light. There are many saints in heaven who will never see God. There are many of the angels that have not seen Him, until Christ Our Lord stepped out of God as flesh.

That is why all the heavenly host were there in Bethlehem. Most of the heavenly host were looking at God for the first time. Whereas the pure in heart, those who have graduated, those who have been purified, purged by fire to a certain level will be able to see through that unapproachable light. Because their character will be compatible to His, causing them to married

161

to Him – to be one with Him.

One of the joys of being married will be to finally see our Bridegroom's face in the full radiance of His glory, no longer turning His glory down. Christ the Lord is in heaven right now and most of the saints' dwell in the outer court – furthest away from His throne. He visits them as the Son of Man. But those who reside in the Holy of Holies see Him as He really is. So, why would we not want that – to see the full radiance of His face, knowing this side of the grave that Christ Our Lord died so that we may walk with Him, Who dwells in unapproachable light?

To not grow in love is to fall short of His eternal redemptive plans for us. This is why when He wipes away tears in heaven, those memories are removed, as well as, we lose the opportunity to follow the Lamb wherever He goes. This is what Christ Our Lord is talking about how the pure in heart shall see God.

Matthew 5:9 (NKJV)

Blessed are peacemakers, for they shall be called the sons of God.

In verse nine, Christ Our Lord says, "Blessed are the peacemakers, for they shall be called the sons of God." Sons are the ones who have matured. They are the ones who carry the peace of God on them. Every place they go, they release peace as Christ Our Lord did. He released the power of peace and it came over the people. This is what is going to happen to the sons of God, those who mature on the earth. Wherever they go, they will bring peace to those who are troubled. They will bring peace to the planet. The planet groans right now waiting for the manifestation of the sons of God.

The earthquakes, tsunamis and asteroids are all because of a lack of peace and the planet is aching on the inside for redemption to come. It needs the peace that we are to carry.

Matthew 5:10

Blessed are those who are persecuted for righteousness' sake, for theirs is the kingdom in heaven.

Blessed are those who are persecuted. When we listen to some Christians talk, we would think He meant cursed – not persecuted. But any place that the enemy is trying to steal from us, it is because we took a stand for truth. Any challenge to our walk – any struggle to obey God, we are being persecuted for righteousness' sake. Even if that persecution is coming from our own flesh, we are still being persecuted. So blessed are those who are persecuted for righteousness' sake! Christ Our Lord further says, "For theirs is the kingdom of heaven."

James 4:6

But He giveth more grace …

Grace is not only favor, but it is God's power as well. For God to give us favor and power, He has to give us revelation. Peter said, it is multiplied unto us through the knowledge of God and of Christ Our Lord. So in giving us revelation, there is an aspect of our soul that must be enlightened. I want to end this summary emphasizing this very important point. To lay these foundations in our lives it will be challenged by the tares or weaknesses in our lives. This is where we will rise or fall as a believer, we must overcome all the hindrances the enemy will attempt to use against us from our own soul.

If we are in need of a breakthrough, it is not just angels coming to push back on something so we can be free from what has been holding us captive. There is an aspect of revelation that must come to us that enables us to be truly free. It comes to our spirit first, causing a reaction from our spirit man on the inside because in that grace there is a power that is released inside of our soul and within our body. So there needs to be an ingrafting of our soul to get that revelation that our spirit is carrying, so that our spirit, soul and body can come into agreement.

God resists the proud but gives grace, favor and power unto the humble. And if there is not an apparent breakthrough in our lives, then it is going to be a challenge for us to humble ourselves before God and before others. In other words, in the midst of the struggle that is going on, He wants us to forget what is at stake. So He messes with our minds and gets us off our game. The Bible says that we should not let these things slip. It is the same way when we are under attack, we have to start taking certain spiritual precautions. Is any among you afflicted? Let him pray. So that is the first spiritual precaution that we need to take. When we fail to do certain things, we bring destruction to ourselves because we do not understand the season that we are in, and the help that we need. If we are under attack and the struggles of life are pressing in, it is because the enemy has legal access or there is sin in our lives. The difficult hard times, whether they are inner struggles or outer struggles, God has permitted it!

Roots Deal with the Source of Our Weaknesses

The difficult times help us to maintain a certain level of humility, so we can get revelation from God so we can hear clearly. So, we can maneuver through what we are going through, His way. In the revealing of that revelation many times God will show us roots that need to be plucked up. Roots deals with the cause and source of the weakness in our lives, that He may prune away the dead branches buried within our soul. When the Father is ready to deal with roots in our lives, we will have multiple emotions going off inside of us, because DNA not only holds emotions but it holds memory as well. It will appear we are under multiple attacks, but it is just one attack at the root level. That means God is now after the root and He will let that thing run its course. And the enemy will take that root with everything that is in it and dump all that stuff into our emotions. And at that point, we will feel many things from our past – things that have already happened to us.

Things we remember and things we had forgotten will start coming to our mind. Things will even begin to bombard our dreams, for they are things that are all in our soul. Some things will start messing with our bodies, especially if there is demonic activity or possession. The enemy knows his days are numbered and he knows this is a root level attack to set us free from things that have hindered our growth in walking after the Lord. Now we can crawl under the bed and stick our heads in the sand if we want, but it will only go deeper. With all this going on the enemy will make it seem like the present situation and whoever he is using is the cause of it all, when

165

the problem is really us, our weaknesses. But that is the time to increase our prayer time, recognize what season we are in and pray!

You Must Cooperate with Heaven

He that is going through a test and he that needs wisdom, let him ask of God who gives liberally. Before James said that, he said, "Count it all joy when you fall into diverse tests. Knowing that the trying of your faith worketh patience." So we need to ask the Lord, "What is this – what is going on? Have I missed it? Is it because there is sin in my life?" No, it is not because you have sinned. It is because there is an offense against God on the inside of you, and if it continues it is what has been causing you to sin. But now the Holy Spirit and the Christ our Lord is ready to take the axe to the root. So you must cooperate with heaven, seek His wisdom and the Lord will show you what to do. And during that time remember humility – stay humble. Not staying humble is like jumping out of an airplane without a parachute – you will fail your test!

This is very, very, very important that we keep this in mind – to stay humble, while what is happening to us. Because there must be a level of meekness being displayed in our lives for us to inherit what God has intended for us. We must maintain a level of meekness every time we go through trials, every time we win, every time we overcome situations, for when we do, we will inherit. Sometimes that possession is not apparent yet. Because there are multiple aspects that we may need to deal with before some things are apparent in our lives. But when we walk in meekness, we will inherit every single time and we will not cast away our confidence.

Luke 6:20-23

And he lifted up his eyes on his disciples, and said, Blessed be ye poor: for yours is the kingdom of God.**21** Blessed are ye that hunger now: for ye shall be filled. Blessed are ye that weep now: for ye shall laugh.**22** Blessed are ye, when men shall hate you, and when they shall separate you from their company, and shall reproach you, and cast out your name as evil, for the Son of man's sake.**23** Rejoice ye in that day, and leap for joy: for, behold, your reward is great in heaven: for in the like manner did their fathers unto the prophets.

Too many Christians are ignorant of the enemy's devices and do not know heaven's ways. These are the foundations that God is endeavoring to build on the inside of us. To make us a wall that is impenetrable by the evil schemes of the wicked one, so that we can be vessels that will be filled with His glory!

* * *

Made in the USA
Columbia, SC
29 October 2021

47972823R00117